THE SEVEN WORLDS
OF THE MINISTER

Gerald Kennedy

THE SEVEN WORLDS OF THE MINISTER

Harper & Row, Publishers

New York, Evanston, and London

Unless otherwise noted, all Scripture quotations
are from the Revised Standard Version.

This is for the preachers of the Los Angeles Area
of The Methodist Church

CONTENTS

PREFACE

It is of great interest to me personally though of practically none to other people that twenty years ago my first book was published by Harper & Brothers. *His Word through Preaching* was a discussion of the preparation and delivery of sermons as well as an attempt to suggest the main themes which ought to underlie the Christian message. I was more sure of my own ideas in those days than I am now but my interest in the subject has grown with the years rather than decreased. In 1947 I assumed that I would be a Methodist preacher for the rest of my life, and since I regarded this as the highest calling God gives a man, I was happy and content.

The Church directed my life into some channels I had not foreseen, but it has not lessened my enthusiasm for the Christian ministry. As a Bishop of The Methodist Church since 1948, I have been close to many churches and many preachers and have had a chance to observe a variety of ministers. I expect my point of view is a little broader today than it was then, or at least it ought to be. There are some things about the minister's task which appear more significant now when viewed from the perspective of 1967. I have a deeper appreciation for the fullness of our task and for the importance of certain phases of it which in the beginning were seen dimly. I still hold to the priority of preaching with the same uncompromising tenacity. But I am more willing now to recognize the necessary part played in the Church by ministers who are not the most able preachers.

It has been a privilege to be assigned to tasks which have broadened my point of view of the Church without removing me from it. The Methodist episcopacy is not an academic retreat and it is no ivory tower. I preach more than ever and for the past twenty years have been in close contact with more than 500 churches and with more than 800 ministers. To some extent I have been responsible for institutions and men and I have been responsible to them. Unlike the board secretary who must promote a particular program, it is the whole work of the Church for which my office is held accountable.

This book is written to bear witness to the wonder of the ministry and to speak some convictions about it. It is written at a time when voices from within and without the churches are crying pessimism. It is written at a time when younger preachers, especially, are sure that they are facing a brand new situation which the Church has never faced before. It is very hard to make them believe that this has been true of every generation of ministers and that so many of the things they regard as radical and new are as old as the Book of Acts.

Perhaps today there is a little more insistent cry that our work is in vain and that the institution is tottering. I say it may be so, but in any case, it is only a matter of degree. My own feeling is that to many people the Church always seems to be tottering and to the critics that Christianity seems always to be in its last days. The prophets of doom do not impress me very much because their continual gloomy predictions have created in me a kind of hopeful contempt. I have listened to their Cassandra prophecies all my life and hardly ever were their grim forebodings realized. Something always happens which their little faith could not discern. Bishop Joseph Butler in *The Analogy of Religion* written in 1736 said: "It has come, I know not how, to be taken for granted, by many persons, that Christianity is not so much as a subject of inquiry; but that it is, now at length, discovered to be fictitious. And accordingly they treat it, as if, in the present age, this were an agreed point among all people of discernment; and nothing remained but to set it up as a principle subject to mirth and ridicule, as it were by way of reprisals, for having so long interrupted the pleasure of the world." You will remember, of course, that this was the period when the Wesleyan Revival was born.

An angry young Catholic critic writes a book about his "outdated church" and says about its preaching: "Recently I made a survey of the sermons in thirty different parishes in five separate states, listening to an average of four sermons in each parish. The results of my study—however modest—are appalling. Frequently I was scolded, even insulted, and most of the time I was talked down to."* What hath the Vatican Council wrought! My Catholic brethren will discover that such criticism is a part of the price of renewal.

If there is one main thesis in this writing, it is that what a good many people complain about as being the weakness of the minister's task is really its strength. He plays many parts and at different times he has varied responsibilities. He will be stronger at some of his jobs than others but he ought to rejoice that like the men of the Renaissance, he is called

---

* James Kavanaugh, *A Modern Priest Looks at His Outdated Church*, Trident, 1967.

upon to be complete. I have divided these various functions into "worlds" but, of course, these are flexible boundaries and the atmosphere of one fades into that of the others. Just for the sake of consideration one has to label them, but we should not assume that these separate categories are to be regarded too seriously.

Ours is an ecumenical age, for which we should all give thanks to God. It troubles me sometimes that this is interpreted to mean that we can substitute abstraction for the concrete. That is, there is too often a tendency to trade the reality of the local congregation, its organization and its minister, for a union of a church and a ministry with no roots in a neighborhood and no foundation on solid ground. My conviction is that nothing is real until it is local, and the coming great Church must find the people where they are and minister to them under the guidance of a man chosen to serve in this particular parish. As Shakespeare put it, "imagination bodies forth," and to its visions the poet gives "a local habitation and a name." Which is what the local minister does when God has touched him.

My chief conviction is that the Christian ministry is more relevant today than ever and that the Christian minister is always where the action is. I have grown weary of hearing counselors tell the wives of young preachers that they must be on their guard against the parishioners of their church lest they be taken advantage of and lose their individuality. I am also sick and weary of pontifical voices from men who never served a church or if they did, never made a success of it, telling young ministers of all the pitfalls of the profession. That there are hard and tragic experiences within the ministry, I will not deny, but that the rewards and adventures of it are so wonderful as to make us forget the tragedies, I do affirm. If any young minister should read this and then say to himself, "It must be a wonderful thing to be a minister, after all," then I shall be content.

The substance of five of the chapters in this book were delivered as the Edwin E. Voigt Lectures at McKendree College in January, 1968. It was a pleasure and an honor to be on that campus.

GERALD KENNEDY

Hollywood, California

THE SEVEN WORLDS
OF THE MINISTER

I THE PREACHER

Soon afterward he went on through
cities and villages, preaching and
bringing the good news of the kingdom
of God.—Luke 8:1

Let me begin by describing briefly the three
convictions which undergird what I want to write. This
seems to me only fair and it may save some readers from
going any further. At least it will reveal the "stance," to use
the present jargon, from which I view the contemporary ministry. If these convictions appear to be prejudices to some, at
least we will have some basis of exercising judgment on the
conclusions.

One, I am a churchman. I believe in the Church and its
necessity for the creation and maintenance of a Christian society. My ministry has now extended over thirty-five years
and any illusions with which I may have started have long
since been destroyed. The modern critics do not shock me
because, frankly, I could take off where most of them stop. I
just thank God that these brethren do not know any more
about the Church than they do. But in spite of all this, I
believe in the Church and I am confident that it will be

preserved until the end of time and that it is essential to the realizations of our Lord's Kingdom.

Two, I am a Methodist preacher and certain that the most wonderful job in the world has been entrusted to me. I have no prejudice against other professions and some of my best friends are professors, social workers, business tycoons, doctors, psychologists, scientists. But there is no doubt in my mind that while I might trade salaries with some of them, I would not trade jobs with any of them.

Three, I am an unworthy Christian who believes that the Christian faith is God's answer to human need and human problems. Christianity shines brighter with every passing year and in every new crisis. These three propositions are beyond debate so far as I am concerned, and I see no possibility of anything changing my mind. It is with these underlying assumptions that I begin to write about the worlds of the ministry and register my testimony concerning the preaching part of our task.

What kind of a man ought to be a preacher? Or, perhaps it is better to ask what kind of a man should a preacher be? This is big enough for a whole book, but it must be dealt with here very briefly and inadequately. Since I could not possibly say enough about it, I shall say only that in my judgment the primary thing is that a man should be as nearly as possible, real. It is pretense which is the greatest enemy of the preacher largely because he cannot hide it from discerning listeners. Preaching is the most revealing thing in the world, and eventually even the most obtuse member of the congregation must see the quality of the person who is doing the speaking. Men can cover it up for a long time, and the kindness of laymen as well as their natural tendency to suppose that a minister must be a good man, will keep the four-flusher hidden for some time. But not forever.

A friend of mine who has been in the ministry for many years said what troubled him more than anything else was that so many preachers he knew were really not very religious men. Those of us who have been in this profession for a number of years will know exactly what he meant. It is both amazing and disheartening to meet the number of preachers who have lost and, indeed maybe they never possessed, the sense of being humble servants of greatness beyond description. These are the ones whose eloquence soon or late reveals them to be the noisy gong or clanging cymbal, and unfortunately some of them get away with it for a long time. One of my professors, who was a very great Christian, spoke of being aware of God and his commission but also being aware of ourselves being aware of God. This is the trap. This is the prevailing sin.

I do not believe, however, that such men are the rule but rather the exception. The ministry for the most part is filled with good and honest men doing the best they can to be faithful. They are hardworking men, too, and I have been proud from the beginning to be numbered among them. The weakness of our ministry is hardly ever the weakness of character. While as an administrator it has seemed to me at times that an unusually large number of men go wrong, still in terms of the number of men serving the Church, no profession can rightfully be prouder of the quality of its members than the ministry.

More and more it seems to me that the essential quality in the preacher's personality is what I used to call a sense of drama. This is the indefinable quality that helps a man to help others see and feel the movement, the conflict, the excitement of life. Whatever other philosophies may say about the nature of man and his experience upon earth, the Christian gospel is committed to the human experience as a battle,

a struggle, and a call to heroism. This is the essential difference between the gospel and a philosophy, for the teaching of
Jesus in the New Testament is not about ideas as ends in
themselves, but about attitudes which are rooted in experience. The Gospel of Mark shows it supremely, but even the
Fourth Gospel which is more contemplative still has at the
heart of it the excitement of decision and action. We should
never forget that the Apostle Paul was not a man of the study
so much as a man of the road. Indeed, whenever we try to
portray Christianity only as an ideology, we squeeze the juice
out of it and leave only a dry and barren form.

The high school girl who came up to the preacher at the
close of his service and said, "It is so exciting to hear you
preach," expressed the heart of it. Preaching that does not
have that exciting quality in it is at best a secondary activity.
The very idea of "good news" carries with it an assumption
that the messenger will never be a careful man objectively
stating a proposition. He will be, on the contrary, a man
shouting a headline. He will be a kindling man whose faith
will fan into flame the smouldering embers of other men's
faith.

Unlike the actor, the preacher writes his own material.
When we consider that the top TV personalities with the
best writers money can buy, run out after a year or two, we
shudder at our own responsibility. Yet it is not quite like
that, after all. We preach an Event and a Presence. And if
God has given us an experience of Christ, it is an inexhausti-
ble spring within us inspiring, illuminating, and revealing.
The preacher discovers that he has been given a magic eye
which reveals the wonder of commonplace stuff. If he pos-
sesses this gift, his preaching is the bread of life.

The laymen of the churches understand this very well, and

more times than I can remember a layman has said to me, "Can't you teach these young preachers to be enthusiastic?" My answer is always the same, "No, I cannot do it because if God has been unable to fill them with the wonder of the message, I certainly do not know how to go about it." But I know what the laymen are saying, and it is a fatal lack for the preacher to be either unable or unwilling to kindle enthusiasm for the Way. If we lack this quality, it would seem to me that we must wait upon the Lord for it until hopefully one day we shall cry out as Bushnell did, "I have found it. I have found the gospel."

Says the popular psychologist, George W. Crane, speaking to preachers, "Yet many clergymen couldn't rate even a 'D' in any high school public speaking class! You are an ally of satan if you drive parishioners away from church by your stodgy public speaking methods." This, of course, has truth in it because some of the dullness springs from poor presentation and an ignorance of even the elementary principles of communication. But finally it is in the quality of our own experience and the condition of our own imagination where the answer is found.

A bishop dropped in unexpectedly to hear one of his young preachers one Sunday morning. The service ended and the two of them sat together in the study. The bishop remarked that the young man must be tired and that he ought to rest for a little while. When the young man replied that preaching never made him tired, the bishop answered, "Son, when a man preaches, somebody gets tired." While it is no sure sign that weariness is a guarantee of effectiveness, you can be certain that effective preaching will so drain a man's emotional strength that he will feel utterly wrung out at the end.

This quality of excitement is much more important than a short sermon. There are preachers who think that weariness is just a matter of length. Let us remember that John Newton heard Whitefield preach, and after a three-hour service he reported, "At the end, I went away rejoicing." It is quite possible to listen to a man speak ten minutes and be bored to death, and to hear another man speak an hour and wish that he would go on.

A preacher, when asked about one of his colleagues, replied, "He is a bright man and has lots of ideas, but there is no movement to his mind." This may express the heart of the situation. Thoughts that do not move and do not lead anywhere are not very interesting. Services that seem to be bogged down in endless contemplation with no final objective to be obtained are tiresome. Preachers who give their whole outline away at the beginning with no promise of advance and no hint of surprise, will not thrill the listeners. When Newton spoke of great crowds attending Whitefield's tabernacle at five o'clock in the morning, it was not only a different generation from ours but must have been an experience full of drama.

Victorian sermons sometimes resembled ministerial filibusters. John Angell James, who was a famous minister in Birmingham, once delivered a sermon of two hours from memory. At the end of the first hour when he asked permission to pause for a moment, members of the congregation threw oranges into the pulpit to refresh him. One of my colleagues preaching to a congregation in Africa a few years ago finished his sermon and then was astounded when the representatives from the congregation respectfully asked him to preach another sermon. None of this is characteristic of our time, but the idea which some people have that interest is created entirely by the shortness of the sermon misses the point.

I add another quality which is very important for the preacher, and that is the ability to learn. There seems to be something about this office which closes the mind to criticism of the way the art is practiced. One of the most disillusioning things in my episcopal experience has been the realization that the man who makes certain mistakes in his first appointment to a church will probably be making the same mistakes in his last appointment. Perhaps we are no worse and no better than men in other professions, but we ought to be better. Yet, this stubborn refusal to accept criticism is so characteristic of my own nature that I do not speak of this weakness with scorn but only with sympathy. One of the most important characteristics of the man whose preaching is to become increasingly effective is the ability to believe that what seems so clear to him may not be clear to the congregation. It is a fine thing when laymen say of a preacher, "He has grown."

In 1834 Henry Sellers, who was the brother-in-law of Bishop John Emory of The Methodist Church, told Matthew Simpson that he must stop putting an "uh" on the end of so many of his words. Simpson, instead of resenting the criticism, reported to Sellers every Monday morning to go over the sermon with him. This may have been one of the reasons he became a great preacher and one of the best known bishops of our Church. But in the beginning, one of the bishops remarked about him, "I heard Professor Simpson preach and it was only a tolerable performance." Men may be born with the potential but the realization of it depends to a large degree on willingness to listen to honest criticism and follow intelligent advice. The minister needs to read with personal heart-searching the biblical word that pride is the supreme sin and humility an essential virtue. Woe unto us when the learning attitude of the little child departs from us and we assume that we have achieved a condition which is final.

A MESSENGER

It will help the preacher to keep in mind always that he is a messenger. Something has been said and something has been done, and we are commissioned to proclaim it to the people. Such an attitude frees us from too much introspection and too much confidence in our own skill and wisdom. Of course, we cannot separate the message from the man, but the fundamental thing is always the message and not the man.

This idea of the preacher as a messenger will save us from some of the horrible concepts which modern men have of the ministry. We will no longer think of ourselves as called upon to be the promoters of a psychological approach to personal problems. This may enter into some of the things we say, but this kind of preaching always deteriorates into little manipulations which lose sight of the majesty of the gospel. If we are messengers we will be kept aware that at the center of our presentation there has to be testimony of what God has done. Nor will we ever escape the truth which is fatal when it is forgotten, that at the center of our good news there is an historical event. I think sometimes of how much better off theology would have been through the years if it had never lost sight of this simple but essential truth.

Yet the sheer magnitude of the task will frighten us especially when we begin. John Bright, the English statesman, said, "Nothing that I can think of would induce me to under-

take to speak to the same audience once a week for a year."
Well, that is a fair warning, and in every subject except the
gospel, it is probably a wise observation. But the strange
thing about this Word we are to preach is that it seems to
renew itself and expand itself with every added year of our
life and with every new experience that comes to us. Actually, the folder where themes for sermons are kept will grow
larger if we keep up our reading and our study. There is an
unseen spring at the bottom of the well which never runs dry
and maintains the water level no matter how much we take
out. As a man grows older his problem is not so much one of
how he is going to find enough to say to get him through
another year, but a happy melancholy that sees the years slip-
ping by so fast with so many wonderful themes not yet developed about the unsearchable riches of Christ.

Still, we must not minimize this and the preacher must
develop the homiletical mind which will see sermons not
only in stones but on the billboard, in the press, and every
time a man talks with him. There is a passage in *The Goncourt Journal* for Tuesday, April 8, 1862, where it is noted:
"Dined with Charles, who told me that Hugo always has a
note-book in his pocket and that if, in conversation with you,
he happens to express the tiniest thought, to put forward the
smallest idea, he promptly turns away from you, takes out his
note-book and writes down what he has just said. He turns
everything into copy or munitions. Nothing is ever lost: it all
goes into some book or other. He has brought this system to
such a pitch of perfection that his sons, who live in hopes of
using what they hear him say, are always beaten to it: whenever one of their father's books comes out, they see all the
notes they have been taking in print." The preacher's mind
has to resemble Hugo's.

THE SITUATION

It is apparent to anyone who thinks about the subject that preaching is at a low ebb today. This is not only in its quality but in the attitude ministers take toward it. One can read all kinds of nonsense about the day of the preacher being over and the Church now turning to other ways of maintaining itself and proclaiming its message. This kind of talk, however, is taken seriously only by young men with limited experience or men with very poor memories. When somebody says to me that preaching is on its last legs, I want to reply, "Brother, it is always on its last legs."

Queen Victoria, returning home from church on Sunday and having found the sermon inadequate, said to the prime minister, Lord Melbourne, "There are not many good preachers." The prime minister, who was not enthusiastically religious but who took a realistic view of things, replied, "There are not many good anything." Not many good preachers, and not many good lawyers either, and for every good one, many shysters. There are not many good doctors, I suppose, and for every outstanding one, a hundred merely mediocre. Maybe that is why doctors are such poor patients.

When I was a student at the theological seminary many years ago, there was a minister from New York City who was pleading for a twenty-five-year moratorium on preaching. Someone during that time predicted with great assurance that with the coming of the radio, we might expect a half dozen or so outstanding preachers to take care of all the pulpits of the nation. The rest of the brethren would be assigned to more menial and less demanding work.

I do not deny the criticism that is being made today, but

the idea that this is something new is childish. The miracle of the Church is that it can grow and be maintained against great odds through the work of very ordinary men. Indeed, the situation in its ministerial leadership is worse than I thought it was twenty years ago. Yet, in every past generation when wise men were turning to something besides preaching to save the Protestant church, men have listened but still come back to this foolish thing which somehow is an inevitable and essential part of the very nature of the Christian faith. Catholicism is turning now toward this New Testament affirmation.

The laymen who talk to me about the needs of their churches do not say that what they need above everything else is a better administrator. This is important but it is not central. They do not ask to have a pastor appointed, although pastoral work is of the utmost significance, as I shall point out later. They do not ask for a counselor or an educator. They say to me, "Can't you send us a preacher? We have been without one for so long and surely we deserve one now." The layman's judgment is sound because he knows, while looking into his own heart, that a church's life goes up or down according to the preaching in the pulpit.

This is true even in the military service so far as the chaplains are concerned. Here is the real ecumenical ministry which has had very little notice on the part of the ecumenical missionaries. Yet if there is one place where it would seem that the primacy of preaching can be questioned, it would be in the military setting. Surely these men have to deal with personal problems, and their preaching can very easily be a secondary matter. Yet on the preaching missions which I have been engaged in during these past years with the military, time after time the commanding officer would say to me, "Is

there any way to teach these fellows how to preach?" I came
to the conclusion that wherever the Church is, there is the
cry for the preacher.

Christian faith which is an announcement of the suprem-
acy of personality finds that it must bring its truth through
personality, as Phillips Brooks stated so clearly in his famous
Beecher Lectures in 1877. Martin Luther, speaking of God's
Word, said, "If a hundred thousand Christs had been cruci-
fied and no one said anything about it, what use would that
have been? Just betrayal to the cross. But when I come to this
we must draw this deed into history and divulge it to the
whole world . . . to the deed must be added the use made of
the deed, that it may be proclaimed by the word, held by
faith and that he who believes may be saved."* To this you
may add the testimony that the event reaches us through
living words of living men passed on from generation to generation. To have written it out would never have been
enough.

So this amazing "truth through personality" comes from
one man who was full of godly fear and from another man
who was full of assurance. It reaches us through the preacher
who is reserved and through the preacher who is all outward
emotion. It comes through slow quiet men and through
quick extroverts. It comes through the man who has a high
attitude of tradition and through the rebel who is all fire. But
there it is, and let us have no more of this nonsense about it
being outgrown or the possibility of finding a substitute for
it.

There are some subjects which can be dealt with adequately through books and written lectures, but preaching is
not one of them. Lectures can be given and much good con-

* Quoted by Gustav Windren in *The Living Word*, Muhlenberg, 1960, p. 65.

cerning the techniques of our craft can be written down. But a living relationship is necessary for us to have the fires kindled in our minds and hearts. The great preacher may be a very poor teacher, but he is a better man to have on the faculty of a theological seminary than the expert pedagogue. For if you hear him and talk with him, you catch a hint of the inner secret of it all which simply cannot be written down.

When Dylan Thomas was asked to discuss his ideas of poetry, he answered, "I am not interested in poetry. I am only interested in poems." The same is true of sermons. The homiletical philosophy is too general, and until a man hears a sermon, the secret of it all will escape him. It is somewhat as Louis Armstrong said when he was asked to define jazz, "Man, if you have to ask you will never know." Emily Dickinson's oft-quoted definition of poetry is to the point as we are thinking of preaching. She wrote, "If I read a book and it makes my whole body so cold no fire can ever warm me, I know that is poetry. If I feel physically as if the top of my head were taken off, I know that is poetry. These are the only ways I know it. Is there any other way?" Probably not.

To put it into the philosophical jargon of our time, the sermon is an existential event. It is one great moment of experience between a preacher, a congregation, and God. When it is over, it is over finally, though it may be written down. But the main element has escaped. Like the newspaperman who does his best and knows that what he has written will be in the ash heap next day or used to line a drawer, so the preacher faces a great moment after hours of preparation, knowing that in about twenty or thirty minutes it is over for good or ill. Yet, he needs to know that in that brief moment great issues may be faced and decided which are eternal in their significance.

Yes, the sermon is certainly an existential event. It is once and forever. It is for this particular moment for better or for worse. This is the great moment when a preacher brings the congregation face to face with decision. Perhaps I feel this more than the man who has a settled pastorate because wherever I preach, I know that the chances are very slim that I shall be back again. At least, if I return it will not be immediately, and I have this half hour to say what ought to be said to the people as a spokesman for the Almighty. This is such a frightening and sobering realization that I run more scared every year.

TECHNIQUES

It is in learning our craft that we can find the most help from one another and from written directions. In this part of our work we need to be patient laborers, learning something about the material and how to use it. Stravinsky, who spoke of the terror that took hold of him when he started to work because everything seemed possible including the best and the worst, wrote these very helpful words: "I shall overcome my terror and shall be reassured by the thought that I have the seven notes of the scale and the chromatic intervals at my disposal, that strong and weak accents are within my reach, and that in all of these I possess solid and concrete elements which offer me a field of experience just as vast as the upsetting and dizzy infinitude that had just frightened me. It is into this field that I shall sink my roots, fully convinced that combinations which have at their disposal twelve sounds in each octave and all possible rhythmic varieties promise me riches that all the activity of human genius will never exhaust."* And we who would preach must come to terms

* *Poetics of Music, in the Form of Six Lessons,* Vintage, 1956, pp. 66-69.

with what we have to work with and discipline ourselves to stay within the limitations. Like the musician, the preacher finds that this is not an enslavement of his genius but a releasing of him to the freedom of his art. These laws of construction and organization, we shall discover, are the road to liberty. Woe unto the man who mistakes license for freedom and so remains ineffective all his life because he never learned the rules of the craft.

Many years ago, Beecher said, "When you have finished your sermon, not a man in the congregation should be unable to tell you, distinctly, what you have done; but when you begin your sermon, no man in the congregation ought to be able to tell you what you are going to do." It is a good word, for the organization of our presentation need not take all the surprise and expectation out of our preaching. What it must do is to make our thought clear and rememberable for our people.

My thought about this part of our work has not changed in all of these years. The plain simple outline with which I began, I have continued to respect, and it seems to me just as important now as at the beginning. You get a few sharp clear points that you want to make about the text, get them arranged in rising significance, and you are almost home. This is the place where we falter and this is the universal complaint on the part of congregations regarding our preaching.

I have a young man in my Conference whom I respect for a certain ingenuity. He found that his preaching was not plain to his people although the outline was clear enough to him. I must say in passing that this is a general experience which makes me labor the point that the outline must be so plain and simple that the wayfaring man need not miss it. None of this complicated, involved stuff which is clear only to us will do. Anyway, this young man decided that since they were not understanding him he would have his outline mimeographed and pass it on to the congregation before he preached. Admittedly, this is a rather desperate measure, but at least it shows the willingness of a man to help his folks follow him. Now if he could just learn to do this so simply that he wouldn't need the outline, he would have achieved the first step of the preacher.

When we work on this skeleton, we must expect to have to do some rearranging and some changing in the order. How many times during these years have I thought it looked good on paper but when I tried to talk it through discovered that something was wrong! Then, suddenly, what seems to be a rather minor change makes the whole thing flow with logic and order.

One of the most interesting books I have read in the last decade is Moss Hart's *Act One*. In it he told of the vicissitudes of a man writing plays for Broadway. He used a very helpful word for preachers. "The big 'hit' of any season always seemed absurdly simple," he writes. "So effortlessly does it unfold, that it almost seems as though it could not have been written any other way. Watch a failure on the same subject, and you will see by what a slim margin the mistakes have been by-passed, the cul-de-sacs averted in the hit."* Later in the book he talks about his experience with *Once in a Lifetime*. Here was the agony of getting something into it that wasn't there and taking something out that should not be there. Finally, he was saved when the producer Sam Harris said to him one night, "I wish, kid, that this weren't such a noisy play." This was the clue, for it was so noisy that it tired everybody out.

I mention this because if anyone thinks that this organiza-

* Random House, 1959, p. 48.

tion business is merely secondary, let him think again. The minor shift here or the small change there spells all the difference between power and mere bombast.

Working on this framework demands a sense of unity and a willingness to be ruthless in our search for it. Ruskin said that unity was everything helping everything else. It is pruning out anything that even hints at getting off the main road. Saint-Exupéry, the French aviator and philosopher who was killed in World War II, put it very well many years ago when he talked about perfection being achieved when there was no longer anything you could take away. To slight this part of our task is as foolish as the men who in some parts of California built houses upon hillsides which were swept away when the heavy rains came. The outline is the foundation and this is the place where we shall either win it or lose it. No amount of decoration will ever save a sermon that is not sound in its construction and organization.

John Newton wrote in his diary: "I spoke near an hour and perhaps should have been shorter if I had had more to say. . . . I had no settled view of my subject." How many sermons have I heard read and preached which fall under this criticism? The main difference between the man who now and again strikes a high point and the man who does it week after week lies in his attitude toward this prosaic work of the outline.

THE ART

The word for us here is simplicity, and the fear of it is the end of many a man's pulpit effectiveness. Yet back of the simple speech there has to be a love of the words and of the language and long weary hours of careful preparation. There was a fruit company which advertised, "When thoroughly stewed even an invalid will enjoy our prunes." This as you can surmise is not simplicity but stupidity. The example is the New Testament, and I still enjoy remembering that the Greek of the New Testament was different from the classical Greek. It was referred to as "the Greek of the holy spirit." Quite so, because the Holy Spirit inspired the book which is vulgar in the sense of being the speech of the common people. It was a language that was really spoken, and so it was a language that was really understood.

Once again let us look at Martin Luther, who had such power in his preaching that he became the father of the Reformation. He writes of his experience: "When I preach in the stadt-kirche I stoop down, I do not look up to the Doctors and the Masters of Arts, of whom there are about forty in my audience, but I look upon the crowd of young people, children, the servants, of whom there are several hundreds. To them I preach. To them I adapt myself. They need it. If the Doctors don't care to hear that style of preaching, the door is open for them to leave."* I think of that whenever I read some of the tortured, twisted, obscure utterances of some of the brethren who would launch a new theology or a new liturgy.

The great Casey Stengel, who has been referred to as "an immortal," had an interesting way with language. It was "a kind of rambling semi-doubletalk laced with ambiguous, assumed or unknown antecedents, a liberal use of 'which' instead of 'who' or 'that,' a roundabout narrative—framed in great generalities and dangling modifiers."† You scarcely could find a better description of much theological talk in

* Nuelsen, *Luther: The Leader*, Jennings, 1906, p. 223.
† Joseph Durso, *Casey: The Life and Legend of Charles Dillon Stengel*, Prentice-Hall, 1967.

our time. Here is an example of Stengelese:

"That feller runs splendid but he needs help at the plate, which coming from the country chasing rabbits all winter give him strong legs, although he broke one falling out of a tree, which shows you can't tell, and when a curve ball comes he waves at it and if pitchers don't throw curves you have no pitching staff, so how is a manager going to know whether to tell boys to fall out of trees and break legs so he can run fast even if he can't hit a curve ball?"

All you can say about this for sure is that it has something to do with baseball. And all you can say about some preaching is that it seems to be in the general field of religion. To say plainly what we mean is a central part of the preacher's art and too often neglected, probably because it is hard work.

On this subject, perhaps, I am thinking too much of the Methodist heritage. Yet this is a part of my Church which seems to me to be eminently worth emulating. The Wesley hymnbook, written mostly by the four Wesleys (the father and three sons), was marked by a wide concern and a heart-reaching directness with the "simple words of agony or exultation." John Wesley had no admiration for artificial eloquence. He said one time, "I am sick and tired of hearing some men preach Christ. Let but a pert, self-sufficient animal, that has neither sense nor grace, bawl out something about Christ or his blood, or justification by faith, and his hearers cry out, 'What a fine gospel sermon.' " Not for him the empty arousements without direct meaning and simple truth. The gospel demands verbs of action and not many adjectives. At least we should use them very sparingly.

The contrast comes home to us when we compare lodge rituals with the simple speech of the Book of Common

Prayer. How artificial and stilted are these sentimentally eloquent monstrosities of the English language, especially when they are read by men not trained to read and not very good readers either.

A few years ago when I came to Los Angeles it seemed important to me that I should know the laymen. A series of meetings was set up for me to meet with them on an afternoon and evening and with no other minister present. They talked freely and openly about their churches and their ministers, and one thing became so clear to me that it made a very great impression. There was almost a unanimous confession that while they knew that the preachers were talking about something vaguely religious on Sunday morning, the exact meaning of their thought hardly ever reached them. Preachers tend to talk in a self-conscious jargon and make references to things familiar to them but to no one else. Whenever a man can talk simply and plainly about Christ, people will come up and with a kind of wonderment on their faces say, "I understood you." The small words, brethren, and the simple words were good enough for our Lord and they ought to be good enough for us.

The art of our preaching demands that we have as little interferences with our communication as possible. This means that preaching without notes is always to be preferred. However, there are differences of opinions about this, and some men will do it one way and some another. But I have yet to meet the layman who will disagree with a man who suggests that speaking without either manuscript or notes is to be preferred.

When Wesley preached the funeral service sermon on George Whitefield's death, he made a rather unusual comment. He said, "It was the 29th [December] that he first preached without notes." Wesley assumed apparently that this was worth noting as one of the great events in the life of the great preacher. If I should write down some of the significant times in my own life, I think the day when I decided to be free of manuscripts and notes in my preaching would be something to be remembered. For every young preacher should decide deliberately and objectively what form his presentation should take if it is to be the best, and he should learn to do it that way and never depart from it.

The social and the personal elements of the gospel must be combined in every sermon. It is no use to preach today on a social issue and say I will have a chance later on to speak to men's personal needs. The man with the broken heart and the woman with the broken dream will not be back again, and if the gospel has a healing word for them, let it be said now. The challenge of social justice will not delay, and so we ought to have in our minds the social and the personal elements in what the Christian faith has to say at this particular time and in this particular place.

Because abstract preaching is poor preaching, we must always come to the concrete if our people are to be grasped by the truth. This means that our illustrations are a most significant part of our art. They are not just a series of stories, and they are never ends in themselves. They are a manifestation of the general in particular situations.

It is a commonplace that the illustration ought to fit the congregation. But there is no greater disaster that can overtake a man than to pretend to know about something which somebody in the congregation really knows, and the preacher does not know. Let the preacher be found out in one phony story and he will be the victim of what has been called the fallacy of the thirteenth stroke. Which is to say that if a clock strikes thirteen, you will not trust it again no matter what it strikes. There is no place where absolute honesty is more necessary than here, and, indeed, Dean Hodges said one time, "When preaching in the country, take your illustrations from the city; when in the city take them from the country. It's safer." He probably meant that under these conditions you will not be tempted so much to claim to know what you do not know. This pushing and pulling of illustrations to make them fit is disastrous. If there is not a natural application, then you have the wrong illustration. You had better wait until you are preaching on something where this is the right word.

After all has been said and done and each analysis has been made as accurately as possible, there still remains an indefinable moment in this preaching task that fills our hearts with wonder. We may do all kinds of things to enrich the service. We can change the furniture and move the pulpit from the center to the side. But the preacher is the element which makes all these things quite secondary. The man called to this task will never doubt that if he has been honored by the call, he has also been driven to a task with such demands as to keep him forevermore humble and filled with a sense of inadequacy.

The older I grow the more the Bible comes to be the great book for the preacher. It is not just a matter of picking out biblical doctrines and proclaiming them. It is certainly not just telling scriptural stories in your own words which some of the brethren seem to assume is the meaning of biblical preaching. It is immersing oneself in the atmosphere of the Bible until that world where God is real and active is your world. It is seeing life penetrated by His spirit and gaining an awareness of being under His orders in every part of one's existence. It is being saved from thinking of religion as a special activity in a special place and seeing the whole of life as the arena where a man is confronted by the Living God.

A little girl, listening to her mother read a Bible story, said, "God was more exciting then than He is now." That is the feeling of a good many people, and that is wrong. God is just as exciting today as He was then, but they understood it and we do not. The preacher is to be for his own time and his own people the man who can make apparent God's presence and God's action in such a way that the Bible becomes contemporary. Said William Russell Maltby, a Methodist preacher of a past generation:

> I who have given to Thee my best
> Rejoice Thy word is unexpressed
> And inexpressible must be.

Quite so, and we shall never cross that barrier. But the hint of this mystery of the reality of God is what the Bible succeeds in communicating, and we must live in it until something of that same ability comes to us.

For fifteen years I preached once a year at the Unitarian Church in Germantown, Pennsylvania. After the death of William Sullivan, a Catholic priest who left his church and finally became a Unitarian minister, the church turned the pulpit into an ecumenical platform and invited men of all traditions and denominations to be the preachers week after week. On my way to the Board of Missions of my Church, I stopped off there at least one Sunday each year and that congregation became very dear to me. The pastor of the church, the Rev. Max Daskam, now retired, had a mimeographed sheet prepared which he sent out to preachers who were coming to the pulpit for the first time. Under the part which he called *The Sermon,* he had written these words: "Ordinarily we never make any suggestion as to your sermon. This is a free pulpit and we want you to preach what is in your heart and mind. Sometimes, however, our guests not knowing our church give a lecture on current events. I well remember one of our loveliest members, doomed with cancer, coming to church for her last time, eager for some word of deep faith, only to have the minister spend his whole time on McCarthyism.

"Preach to us, then, as you would to any congregation. Do not pull your punches. Blast McCarthy or any wrong or injustice as you will. But above all, speak to us of the deepest spiritual faith your heart holds. We need to be put back on the track of things eternal."

I read that over from time to time to remind me of what the sermon is. Only if you think that men are no longer in need of this can you believe that preaching has come to a dead end. Since all my experience and conversation assures me that men need to be set back on the track of things eternal as much and perhaps more today than ever before, I am confident that the preacher is called for such a time as this. I am confident also that this part of the minister's calling is more wonderful and awful with every passing year.

II   THE ADMINISTRATOR

And God has appointed in the church . . .
administrators. . . .—1 Corinthians 12:28

On a journey around the world in 1960 with
Bishop G. Bromley Oxnam, we visited the Ecumenical Patriarch in Constantinople. At a Sunday luncheon he gave for us
we talked about the service we had just attended in the
cathedral. The Patriarch said that it was too long and that
there was pressure to have it shortened, especially from the
young people. I asked him when the last change in the service
had been made, and he replied, "The eighth century." I
asked him why they did not shorten the service, and he said
such an action would demand an ecumenical conference. I
was persistent and asked why they did not call one, and his
reply was, "We are not quite ready."

In contrast with that spirit, I thought of my communion
which meets every four years to tamper not only with the
machinery, but even with the ritual. If we go too far and too
fast in this direction, certainly the Orthodox Church was not
moving fast enough; and in some way, each body of Christians ought to keep the machinery of the organization effective for the day in which it is operating. This, I take it, is the
purpose of administration.

In the seventeenth century, Lord Falkland, who had a great sense of the importance of tradition, pronounced the formula for change in these words: "Where it is not necessary to change it is necessary not to change." This may sound like a reactionary point of view, but rightly understood it is a helpful generality. He was saying that we ought not to change just for the sake of change. Just because a thing is new does not mean it is automatically better. If an organization is working, stay with it, and in any case, never discount the importance of tradition and experience. Lord Falkland was, in other words, stating the case for conservatism.

Now most people, apparently, feel that administration is at best a necessary evil in the Church. It is a necessary part of any human institution, but the minister must be expected to resent it. One can attack church administration without hearing any rebuttal, but on the contrary, the critic will be regarded as a prophet speaking out bravely against the machinations of the priest. For a man to like administration seems slightly scandalous.

There was a time when I was a member of this large company, but no more. The passing years have given me an increasing appreciation for the administrative part of our ministry, though I must confess I am not very good at it and I do not particularly enjoy it. This appreciation is probably due to my responsibility as a bishop. But I hope it is due also to a larger and more realistic view of the Church. My change of attitude began a good many years ago in the Northwest when I observed a young and brilliant preacher in a church that was badly located and so rundown that it was an eyesore in the community. His idea of building a new church was to have a five-dollar banquet every year for the building fund. I calculated one time that at the rate he was going, it would be about thirty years before he would have enough money to break ground for a new edifice. When he moved and was appointed to another church, I sent a man there who was not nearly the brilliant preacher his predecessor was, but he was a man who could draw the water and hew the wood of administration. In less than a year there was a financial campaign organized and under way, and in a little more than a year, ground was broken for a new church which was finished under his ministry.

That experience told me that there are men who will never shine as great pulpit masters, but they will serve the Church in their own way. It would be wrong, I am sure, to assume that the good administrator can eliminate the need for the good preacher, but we ought to see the Christian Church as in need of men who have some skill in this field and every minister ought not to despise this part of his labor.

There came to my desk some time ago a small newspaper entitled "The Union Priest," and underneath it, "The Official Publication of the American Federation of Priests." I learned on reading through the paper that this is an organization started by a rebellious Catholic priest to exercise pressure and power against the institution of the Roman Catholic Church. Right out in the open is the assumption that the Church is an organization and the employees of that organization have to be organized. All of this seems quite wrong to me, although I am not so naïve as to assume that I will never have to deal with it in my communion. I believe, however, that this is witness to a failure of administration at some point. But may the good Lord forbid that the Church shall ever come to a place displaying to the world another battleground where the wars of management and labor are fought before the public. This is simply an indication of how important it is for the laity and the professional people within a church to learn and to practice sound principles of administration which are Christian and democratic. For a few sensitive, self-consciously spiritual ministers to despise the whole affair does not seem to me an intelligent answer to the problem.

President Elliott of Harvard said one time that the most necessary quality for an administrator was the ability to inflict pain. I understand that saying and so will any minister who has to hurt somebody's feelings in order to open the way for church activity and church witness. But the ministry was never meant to be free from pain, and we have no right to let our churches stagnate because we lack the courage or the will to do the practical and necessary thing.

On February 9, 1877, Phillips Brooks preached an evening consecration service sermon at Trinity Church, Boston. He said: "The church has new standards, new ambitions, new ideas of work. This is the modern notion of a church, not luxury, but work. God help us to cast off everthing old and avoid everything new which can keep us from doing perfectly that great work which we can hear our Lord calling her to do for Him." This sums up the task of the administrator in words as relevant today as they were a hundred years ago. This is our purpose and this is our task.

The job of being responsible for a Christian church in our day is just about the hardest job any man is called to do. I do not know any responsibility that seems to me to be more demanding of so many talents. My friend, J. Wallace Hamilton, long-time minister of a Methodist church in Florida, puts it this way: "The modern preacher has to make as many calls as a country doctor; he has to shake as many hands as a politician. He has to prepare as many briefs as a lawyer; he has to see as many people as a specialist. He has to be as good an executive as a college president; he has to be as good a financier as a banker; and in the midst of it all, he has to be so good a diplomat that he could umpire a baseball game between the Knights of Columbus and the Ku Klux Klan." Now that we are properly humbled, let us begin to look at this administrative task of the minister.

THE SITUATION

In the present time the administrative responsibilities of the minister have become so great that a good many people think they have reached the breaking point. If you live in the section of the country where I have been working during the past sixteen years, it seems sometimes that the whole job is keeping up with the exploding population. We are called upon to find the funds to build new churches when the process becomes more expensive with every passing year. Men called to preach the gospel find that they are called also to build new sanctuaries until the pressure of this work almost usurps the place of proper study and pastoral visitation. So Professor Joseph Sittler of Chicago speaks about the "maceration" of the minister. He talks about him becoming a promotional man having so many managerial duties that he loses his relationship with God. "The will of God has got to be simplified into a push for the parish house," he writes. "The Holy Spirit is reduced to holy resource which can be used as a punch line for the enforcement of parish purposes. . . . The message, in short, is managed in terms of its instrumental usefulness for immediate goals." This is, indeed, a sad situation but it is greatly exaggerated. There is certainly another side to the story which I hope to make clear.

Still, we must not discount this point of view. When appointing a district superintendent for one of the Methodist districts in Southern California and Arizona, I have sometimes said to him that in all probability he will not learn anything new about the Bible in his six-year term, but he will certainly learn a lot about real estate values. Hopefully, after a few years such a man will be able to point to several places where congregations are working and witnessing and know in his heart that they would not have been there without his personal leadership and work.

One morning in a theological seminary where I was teaching, a professorial colleague came into the room where several of us were enjoying a coffee break. He looked at me and said that he had discovered what was probably the earliest mention of a bishop in Greek history and wondered if I would be interested in hearing of it. Of course I was interested, and he said that from the seventh century B.C. there comes a document which refers to "episcopas," a term which the church has taken over and translated "bishop." "Do you know what he was or do you know what he did?" he asked. I did not know. "Well," he said with some obvious relish, "the episcopas was the straw boss of a road gang." I told him it was about as good a definition as I had heard of my job and it certainly had scriptural foundation. Said Isaiah in his 40th chapter, verse 3:

> In the wilderness prepare the way of the Lord,
> make straight in the desert a highway for our God.

Straw boss of a road gang is what I ought to be. And it is what a minister ought to be as we seek to organize our people to build highways in the desert for our God.

Some ministers will like this part of the work and many will despise it; and each one because of his feeling will be open to certain temptations which he must resist as if they were the devil. The man who likes administration is blessed in some ways, but let him beware lest he neglect the other part of his work and make this a substitute for prayer and study. One of my colleagues, who at one time was my successor, has a great gift in this field. He told me one day that he enjoyed nothing more than conducting a financial campaign or preparing an organizational attack on some particular problem. Imagine! His ministry has been a witness of what great good a man can do who has gifts in administration. There are few churches where more people are at work than in the ones he has served, and there is a smoothness in the relationships which has prevented the congregation wasting its time fighting itself.

This was never my situation. Administration to me is hard work and hardly ever very pleasant. But the years have told me that it is important work, and I must do the best I can with it. I remember the old preacher, listening to a young man complain about not feeling like preaching at certain times, who growled out, "A good deal of the ministry, young man, is doing what you do not feel like doing, and doing it when it ought to be done." My way of handling these responsibilities was to find a layman who was skilled in this particular part of the ministry and laying it upon his conscience to make his contribution through this particular activity. And so there was a time in my first appointment to a little church after seminary when the total budget was about $3,000 and the chairman of the Finance Committee was the president of one of the expanding corporations which has now become one of the giants in our economy. Looking back upon it, it seems so ridiculous and yet so wonderful that this man who dealt in millions served this little church by contributing his skill and knowledge to the financial program.

THE PLACE OF ADMINISTRATION

Cleveland Amory in the *Saturday Review** says that his favorite sign of the month was in the window of a Manhattan store called Petit Musee Ltd. and written by Charles Walker, the store's proprietor. Here are his observations: "An executive has nothing to do—that is except—to decide what is to be done—to tell somebody to do it—to listen to reasons why it should not be done—why it should be done by somebody else—or why it should be done a different way—to prepare arguments and rebuttal that shall be convincing and conclusive—to follow up to see if the thing has been done—to discover that it has not been done—to inquire why it has not been done—to listen to excuses from the person who should have done it—and did not do it—to follow up a second time to see if the thing had been done—to discover—that it has been done but done incorrectly—to point out how it should have been done—to conclude that as long as it has been done—it may as well be left as it is—to wonder if it is not time to get rid of a person who cannot do a thing correctly—to reflect that the person at fault has a wife and seven children—and that certainly no other executive in the whole world would put up with him for another moment—and that in all probability—any successor would be just as bad—and probably worse—to consider how much simpler the thing would have been—had he done it himself—he would have been able to do it right—in twenty minutes—but that as things turn out—he

* Nov. 1, 1966.

himself spent two days trying to find out why it was that it had taken somebody else three weeks to do it wrong—and then realize that such an idea would strike at the very foundation of the belief that—an executive has nothing to do."

This makes clear that being an administrator takes much patience and more time than doing the job yourself. Yet this extra time must be taken because there are religious values in our task and the one-man show never serves the kingdom as well as the organization under a skillful administrator. If we look at the beginning of the Methodist movement, we shall see a very clear illustration of this point. I think there can be no argument as to George Whitefield's superiority as a preacher over John Wesley. Whitefield was a great spellbinder, and he drew tremendous crowds in England and in America. Benjamin Franklin talks about Whitefield addressing a crowd from the steps of the City Hall in Philadelphia, and Franklin estimated there must have been 20,000 people present. Wesley, on the other hand, was never a preacher in that league. But Wesley drew people together in "classes" with someone in charge, so that wherever he preached, he left behind him a fellowship. Out of this rather simple idea there came the class meetings and the framework for what ultimately became The Methodist Church. The solid accomplishments of the evangelical revival in the eighteenth century would not have been possible without this skillful conservation of the results of the preachers.

The moment that one begins to think in terms of organization, the issue of compromise becomes a very real one for him. It is all very well to announce grandly that the end does not justify the means. But when one is working with persons with a shining goal beckoning in his own mind, it is very easy to lose the clear sense of what compromise is. Too far to one

side and he is using persons, which is a sin. If he goes too far
to the other side, he is demanding all or nothing, which turns
the church into an exclusive club. It was put very well by
George Bernard Shaw in a comment on one of his contem-
poraries who had resigned his seat in Parliament rather than
compromise. Shaw wrote: "When I think of my own unfor-
tunate character, smirched with compromise, rotted with
opportunism, mildewed with expediency, blackened by ink
contributed to Tory and Liberal newspapers, dragged
through the mud of Borough councils and Battersea elec-
tions, stretched out of shape with wire-pulling, petrified by
permeation, worn out by twenty-five years pushing to gain an
inch here and straining to stem a backrush there, I do think
Joe might have put up with just a speck or two on those
white robes of his for the sake of the millions of poor devils
who cannot afford any character at all because they have no
friends in Parliament. Oh, these moral dandies, these spiritual toffs! These superior persons! Who is Joe anyway that
he should not risk his soul occasionally like the rest of us?"
You can hardly put the situation of the administrator better.
He stands in need of prayer and he stands in need of a continual sensitivity to his danger.

There are four propositions which the minister as an
administrator needs to keep clear in his mind constantly. (1)
Each man can do something. Sometimes it is rather difficult
to find just what a fellow can do, but we must keep on searching until we discover it. (2) Each man wants to do something. He may not know this exactly, but a good deal of the
criticism and unhappiness in a church comes from people
who are on the outskirts and not actively engaged in some
part of its labor. (3) Each man needs to do something. The
most miserable people in the world are those with no obliga-

tions and no demands upon them. (4) We must believe that there are religious values in administration. This is the answer to all those ivory-tower dwellers who assume that administration is entirely evil and that in some promised land there will be no administration involved for the minister whatsoever. I have known men who have saved other men through their skillful administration.

I hear some very interesting lectures by angry young men who talk about the "house churches" of the New Testament as if that is still the ideal. Believe me, it is not and we are not going to go back to those simple fellowships of our beginnings because the church is different today and so are the times. For better or for worse, the Christian Church operates as an institution, and if you destroy it today, you will have to build it up again tomorrow. That it is fraught with danger is not debatable, but that it can be eliminated and some ancient and informal pattern adopted is nonsense.

Let us not forget that good administration does not mean a great many meetings with no importance and no relevancy. It is sometimes assumed that this is what we are talking about, but, believe me, it is not. The average church can eliminate a vast number of its meetings and no one will be hurt, and none of us ought to allow meetings to be called with no specific purpose. I saw a cartoon some time ago where a man and his wife were looking at a picture of the Last Supper in an art gallery. He says to her, "That reminds me I have a meeting tomorrow." This is the kind of administration that needs elimination.

The Goncourt brothers wrote in their *Journal* for January 24, 1868: "If there is a God, atheism must strike him as less of an insult than religion." Whenever I see some of the useless activities we carry on in the name of the Church or in the name of Christianity, I understand what these words mean. May we be saved from all the useless running around and wasting time considering things that are not important and debating issues which make no difference.

After we have recognized the dangers, then let us come to terms with the proposition that all of us need the pressure of administration. Our Jewish heritage will give us some light here, for the Jewish rabbi and scholar was to learn a trade so that he could do something with his hands. Our Lord was a carpenter and St. Paul was a tentmaker. The Jewish idea held that no man should consider himself an intellectual apart from the life of the people. So when St. Paul was under criticism from the Corinthian church, he could say that he did not take money from them and "did not burden any one" (2 Cor. 11:9). This was his general practice, so that he could write to the Philippians: "And you Philippians yourselves know that in the beginning of the gospel, when I left Macedonia, no church entered into partnership with me in giving and receiving except you only" (Phil. 4:15). The Apostle earned his living by practicing his trade. So the minister is not to be thought of as an "intellectual," and his task is not primarily academic. He is saved from any temptation in this direction by the burdens of administration which the church puts on him and which he ought to bear with as much grace as he can muster.

Who is interested in budgets? Well, only practically every man in the congregation, and to set a religious leader free from this responsibility automatically creates a chasm between him and his people. Years ago in one city where I served, I was at the same time a member of the executive committee of the Community Chest and the president of the Council of Social Agencies. I was the man in the middle, which has been neither the first time nor the last. The Community Chest men were very much aware of budgets and the importance of giving an account of financial responsibility. The social agency people were concerned with programs and took a rather easy view of budgets. They let others worry about such mundane affairs. Both of them were right and both of them were wrong because they needed each other. There is always the end purpose and there is the means to it. The administrator of a church who is a minister finds himself in both positions, and while it does not make him comfortable, it does make him aware.

I have heard businessmen say of a preacher sneeringly, "He never met a payroll." I want always to reply to that kind of statement that the minister has done something even more difficult. As head of an institution depending upon free-will offerings for its life, he has to hold up the cause in such a way that realistic men will think it is worth supporting. A minister is responsible for an institution that is always within one generation of annihilation. And may I say that when one looks at what the churches have done through the years in the way of welfare, missionary, and social services, the record is very good. As a class, ministers are not famous for their financial ability, but as to the record of the institution they serve, they do not need to be ashamed.

There was a time in my ministry when a man suggested that perhaps I could be released from the administering responsibilities of the church and be set free to roam the country preaching. It sounded very good, but deep in my heart I knew it was a temptation I must resist. From time to time there is talk in my church about releasing a bishop from all administrative responsibilities in a particular area. While it has much appeal to me (if I could be the one released), the

Church thus far has been wise to make each one of its bishops responsible for a particular program. In World War II, Winston Churchill would not have an adviser who was not head of a department. The instinct is right that the man who is an adviser ought to be responsible for the practical affairs of a particular section.

TECHNIQUES

In any church it is very important that somebody should be in charge. This does not mean that dictatorial methods will work, but it does mean that every church wants leadership on the part of its minister. It is a most distressing sight to see churches where the laymen are ahead of the minister both in devotion and vision. Laymen will resent it if they think the preacher is running things without democratic procedures and without consultation. This is particularly true of the preacher's wife, who will get into trouble easier by doing too much than by doing too little. Here is a place where great tact is required of the wife who is trained and talented. Let her be the power behind the president of the Woman's Society rather than the president. Let her suggestions be soft and gentle rather than strident. For both minister and wife, a friend of mine has given good advice. He says you have to let them have your way.

This, of course, demands some psychological skill and some tact and understanding. This is very hard to learn, but we must do the best we can. It falls back finally upon imagination, and if I can learn to put myself in the other man's place and ask myself how I would react if he were saying to me what I intend to say to him, I shall be on the right path.

More and more, it seems to me that the quality of confidence in one another is at the base of it all. It is not wise to let a church board get into the habit of saying no. My own suggestion is that the minister should meet with a few of the key laymen and find out how they feel before he brings anything up at an open meeting. This is called manipulation by some, but I believe it is godly manipulation. There is usually in every church a few men whose words carry the most weight. If they are for it, it will go, and if they are not for it, it will probably fail. A man soon learns who these men are, and he can have lunch with them ahead of time and find out how they feel and thus know where he stands so far as the program is concerned.

One of the things that impresses me the most is that the Church as an institution is not greatly different from any other institution so far as the rules of procedure and principles of administration are concerned. As an institution, the Church is as subject to Parkinson's Law, for example, as a government bureaucracy or a business organization. John W. Gardner, formerly president of the Carnegie Corporation and now the Secretary of Health, Education and Welfare in the government, put down a series of principles some time ago which seem to me to have real application for the Church. His nine propositions are worth our consideration, and by applying them to our own organizations, we can find some general guidance.

1. We must have an effective program for the recruitment of the development of talent. It is no good for the same people to serve on the same committees in a church year after weary year. They are good and faithful men, no doubt, but a church had better have some limited term of service on its boards and commissions to which no exception is made. We will lose a good man for a short time, but no man is indis-

pensable. Some of the revolt on the part of young people in the Church is due to their inability to serve and be heard within its structure.

2. There must be a hospitable environment for the individual, and this is particularly true of the Church. It may be true in the city that "you can't fight city hall," but it must not be true in the Church. The minister must be a good listener, and he will spend much time hearing nonsense and opinions based on ignorance. However, now and again he will get a clue of something he has missed and, in any case, the man who talks will feel better.

3. There must be built-in provisions for self-criticism. This is something different from sessions designed to allow troublemakers an opportunity to criticize. It must be more constructive than most of these sessions are. The minister will be well advised to have some group whose business it is to listen to the congregation and to report to him what they hear. It is important to look at the whole organization from time to time and assess its strengths and weaknesses. There is a Turkish proverb: "The man who tells the truth should have one foot in the stirrup." And that applies to most human situations. If the minister can find grace enough to listen to the critics with understanding, it is amazing what a long step forward he will have taken toward good administration.

4. We need fluidity of structure, for a church like other groups tends to specialize too rigidly. Our structures oftentimes are set up to solve problems that no longer exist, and the ability to adjust our organization to meet the present day is too rare. A church business manager spent the best part of two months mimeographing everybody's job requirements and every committee's responsibility. He really accomplished

very little, for every time you have to enlarge the rule book, you are bearing testimony to the decreasing life of the institution.

5. Let us watch internal communications so that the people know what the whole program is and which way we are moving. Most churches are full of people who have not the foggiest notion of any of its life outside the Sunday service. Ministers must be interpreters of the denomination's larger aims and purposes. We need to let the people know where their money is going and what these funds support and accomplish. Obviously, this is not to be done on Sunday morning, but it ought to be done regularly and adequately.

6. We must not become the victims of our procedures. Secretary Gardner told a wonderful story about an officer at Aachen in the last days of World War II. He had been ordered to go to London immediately, but when he went to headquarters, he found they had just moved in and had not established their regular procedures. A sergeant told him that the plane left in thirty minutes, that there would be no other for several days, and that it took twenty-five minutes to get to the airport. The orders which the officer had to have usually took anywhere from two hours to two days to prepare. But the sergeant went back into the other room to see what could be done and came back four minutes later with the orders complete. When he was thanked for his service, the sergeant replied, "Sir, it's just lucky for you we weren't organized." That is what happens sometimes.

Every organization stands in danger of becoming a great clumsy bureaucracy where nothing can be done very soon. The National Council of Churches ought to give a medal to those people who have called it subversive because by making it appear dangerous, it makes it appear relevant. When one learns something about the procedures which the Council thinks are necessary and perhaps are, you wonder why it doesn't fall of its own weight. Let us be grateful for the critics who have saved it by attacking it. Incidentally, it would be a good thing if all the brethren who speak with such starry-eyed wonder about the ecumenical movement and the coming "one Church," would consider how that church is going to function. It will not live in a vacuum. It will have to be organized, and this is what frightens some of the more realistic brethren.

7. The Church like other organizations needs protection against the vested interests. It is disillusioning but it is true that people easily come to believe that they own the church or, at least, their own committees are sacrosanct. One of the main obstacles to overcome if a church wants to grow is the opposition, quiet and unannounced, of certain old-timers who want it just as it has always been. This is why a constant flow of leadership is necessary and why young people must not be shut out.

8. We must keep our eye on what we are to become and not on what we have been. This is, indeed, a good word for the Church. It is the minister's obligation to keep the vision of the future before the people. Living in the past is not confined to church members, but it is certainly one of their prevailing sins. The vision of the Church of the future and the sense of moving toward it step by step will do more to unite a congregation than any other procedure. In these last years we have built a number of new churches out my way, and I have made a very interesting discovery. The very best young men are willing to be appointed to an empty five acres of land and to carry the main responsibility for starting from nothing. They welcome the stimulus of hopes and dreams for

tomorrow. I have talked with them from time to time and inquired what it was like to be pastor of a new church with no past. Almost without exception they have fairly glowed with enthusiasm, and they have told me that the congregation is made up of so many young parents who have lost touch with the churches or have never had any church relationship. These are people who find it new and exciting, and there is never a one among them who can say, "We never did it this way before," or, "We have always done it that way." The task is to create this same spirit in the established church. While this is not easy, neither is it impossible.

9. Finally, the problem in institutions is morale. Dr. Gardner said that men must believe that it makes a difference whether they do well or badly, and this is particularly applicable to the Church. The ceiling is almost unlimited for a group of people committed to an enterprise they believe in and under the spell of a vision they want to make actual. How important it is that men should be proud of their church and should want to tell other people about it. Indeed, this is the only form of church advertisement that I have ever believed was of much value. The vital enterprise always is marked by this spirit within the people.

Somewhere the British novelist, C. P. Snow, has spoken of the quality of having the future in your bones. This is what the Church has, and its history is one long story of static forms suddenly coming to life in new and unexpected ways. The present emphasis on renewal is a part of the tradition. While we may have our disagreements as to just what renewal means and the particular circumstances which will produce it, we can have no disagreement regarding the need of renewal itself.

Just here consider that oft-abused figure of "the organization man." Let me speak a good word for him. He is regarded usually as a man with no individuality who is simply content to find his place within the organization and then play it safe. I have no doubt that there are men like that, and they are sometimes the political wheelhorses who keep the young enthusiasts cooled off and prefer the dull gray atmosphere of mediocrity. We should not assume, however, that this is the whole story. The man who has a sense of great responsibility to the institution is not to be despised, and oftentimes he is a disciplined person who surrenders his own chance to make an impression or a headline for the sake of the fellowship. He knows that the minister is of value to the extent he can carry his people with him. *Time* or *Newsweek* may never put him on the cover, but at the end of the day he is the kind of man who has understood that the Church is the Body of Christ and it is an extension of the Incarnation. He assumes that his personal whim is less important than the church he serves.

Such men have a sense of the past and a sense of what is possible. They do not expect miracles, and they do not expect institutions to act any other way but slowly and deliberately. They know, however, that if the institution does move forward that it has established a new bridgehead which the men of tomorrow may further exploit. These are conservative men in the best sense of that word, and they do protect what ought not to be lost. They have a sense of what must be saved to mark off the starting place for the new advance. A locomotive can go faster by itself, but its task is to pull the train. The locomotive, in other words, is an administrator.

THE ART OF ADMINISTRATION

The minister who takes seriously this part of his work may find it a means of grace both for himself and for his people.

The church which is full of quarreling bitterness is in no position to speak to the world about anything. Let no man, therefore, think administration is an unimportant part of his labor and a small part of his responsibility. The clergy must separate hope from illusion. On the hard anvil of congregational life, the swords must be beaten into the ploughshare to cultivate the Kingdom. To this extent then, the Church is always pragmatic and perhaps my own communion has more than its share of this quality. But Christians are not other-worldly idealists talking about what would be nice. They are men and women who within the bounds of their fellowships are demonstrating to the world how the gospel really works.

THE LAITY

In our day we hear a great deal of talk about the place of the laity in the Church. Men are even writing books about it and creating theologies about it, which seems to me to be making a great noise about an old truth which every minister has been aware of since the first day he became responsible for a church. However, it seems necessary to put it into more sophisticated terms for some of the brethren, and we should rejoice that the truth is percolating down into some churches which find it new and exciting. All of us, however, need to be aware of our responsibility to call each layman to his ministry, which is an idea recovered by the Reformation and actually goes back to the first century.

One mistake of the modern church has been to assume that laymen only do the Lord's work when they become lay preachers. This clutters up a church's work with a lot of second-rate preaching and fills some "professional" laymen with more pride than is good for them. "Laymen's

Day" in most churches simply means a day off for the preacher, and while there are certainly many exceptions, the experience usually is not a very happy one for most people. There are some churches where they stay away in great numbers on this day, apparently preferring to have the professional doing what he has been trained to do. One of my friends remarked one time that he thought this idea of "Laymen's Day" was a good one which ought to be applied to all professions. He said it would be fine to have such a day at the hospital because he said he had always wanted to try his hand at taking out an appendix. This seemed to him to be quite in harmony with the general spirit of the emphasis. We are certainly wrong when we assume that the laity is serving most acceptably when it preaches from a pulpit. No, let the minister in his role as administrator bring every man and woman into a dedication of their talents to the Church in the name of Christ. Let him help each man learn the joy of doing his work both within the Church and out of it as unto the Lord.

A large and most significant part of any church's life is its women. An intellectual has been defined as a fellow who thinks there is something more interesting to talk about than women. Not being an intellectual, let me talk about women in the Church. I saw an article some time ago in an ecumenical magazine with this title, "Women in the Church: A Theological Problem?" I did not read any further, for while I have heard women called many things, I have never heard them labeled a theological problem.

The importance of the distaff side for the Christian Church can hardly be exaggerated. Not that they are completely freed from original sin, but their service and their presence are so significant that the minister learns their value in a short while. Let it not be an attitude of "the ladies, God bless them" or "the women, God help us."

This is one part of the Church where the minister is well-advised to remain somewhat distant. The women are not anxious to be directed or controlled by men so far as their church organizations are concerned, and they do not want to become simply another "ladies' aid" whose chief task is to provide church dinners, especially when the budget is low. Therefore, let the minister offer suggestions when asked—but only then, and within limitations. The "feminine mystique" is a very real factor these days, and probably there is reason for it. It will become obvious to the young preacher in a hurry that the road to harmonious relationships with this part of the church is labeled appreciation and not criticism. A friend of mine went to an important church many years ago, and the first day in town he got into an argument with the president of the Woman's Society of the church. You can imagine how long he lasted! Sooner or later somebody will write a book on "The Theology of the Woman's Society," but until that happens, simply be grateful for the outstanding work the women of the churches do and try to help them to like you.

Many years ago in my first church, I tried the critical approach in dealing with the ladies and I found out in a hurry it would not work. I knew they had forgiven me one Christmas when my salary had not been paid and I received a check from them for $100. That was true love and true Christian forgiveness.

The women of the Church are among the most practical part of the congregation. They know what can be done and they know how to get it done. They will not waste their time in setting up elaborate codes of ethics or fancy systems of theology. They will do more actual work in the community than most any other part of the organization. They are also the most liberal part of the church as a rule. Years ago when we were still struggling in our communion with the racial tensions and prejudices of the Deep South, the women of that section were making their pronouncements about racial justice and having their interracial meetings. Mine has been a growing appreciation of the Methodist women, who are the ones I know the best. And if they have not always done exactly what I would have preferred, they have carried more than their share of the load, and I shall always rise up whenever the opportunity arises and call them blessed.

In 1848 Horace Bushnell wrote in *Christian Comprehensiveness* some very important words for people who were quarreling with each other within the fellowship of his church. Said he: "Thus it may be said that the present distribution in the church, abating what is due to causes that are criminal, makes it more completely one; just as an army sets off into companies and battalions, some to train as infantry and some as horse, some are artillery and some with a rifle, undergoing each a form of exercise and discipline befitted to itself, becomes thereby not several and distinct armies, but because of the orderly distribution made, more complete and perfect whole—in the field, an engine of greater power, because it unites so many forms of action and bears so many sorts of armor." This it seems to me is a good word for the differing parts of the church's life which we cannot and ought not to try to squeeze into one form. Let us allow Christians to express themselves in many different ways and through many different organizations.

Professor Charles M. Neilsen of Colgate-Rochester Divinity School, in a *Christian Century* article discussing the difficulty of Protestantism experiencing the fullness of the corporate Christian life, comes to the end with this prayer: "Dear Lord, we are grateful for all the individualists and gadflys you have sent us. Hermits are interesting, but next time may we please also have a few Benedictines to build, organize and serve the church." And to this I would say an enthusiastic Amen! Ministers will neglect this part of their calling to their sorrow and to the detriment of the Church. If they accept it as significant, if not altogether pleasurable, they may discover that their administrative function will bring them more solid and lasting satisfaction, to say nothing of joy, than they had supposed. At least, this is one of the worlds in which we must live and have our being.

III THE PASTOR

And he said to him, "Lord, you know
everything; you know that I love you."
Jesus said to him, "Feed my sheep."—John 21:17

One of the old-fashioned concepts of the work of
the minister is expressed by the term pastor. Its connotations
are of another age and of another society, for it is definitely
pastoral in its meaning. The pastor is the shepherd of the
flock, and if there is one thing we seem certain of in our time,
it is that modern people not only fail to understand what a
flock is, but they certainly do not want to think of themselves
as part of one. So we have had the "demythologizing" school
of theologians who are sure that new terms have to be found
if we are to speak to an urban and industrialized society. My
own conviction is that most of this talk is nonsense. While
our saying together, "The Lord is my shepherd," is not the
imagery of the city, rather than discarding it, we should explain its richness of meaning for which no substitute can be
found. If we should change our religious terms and imagery
to fit this particular day, what will the future do? Surely no
one should believe that ours will be the final word. My conviction is that people were never more in need of a pastor

than they are in the last half of the twentieth century, and the ministry can never abdicate from this part of its responsibility.

The idea of the minister as pastor of a congregation is unique to the Christian faith. As Professor Charles Ranson of Drew Theological Seminary one time put it, there is no other religion which created such an office, although some other religions have copied it, and there is no other relationship men have in life which corresponds with it. Those of us who have grown up within the Christian Church have assumed that the pastoral function is old hat. It would be a good thing if we would pause for a moment and consider how dramatically different and wonderful it really is. The years of my ministry have increased my respect for the pastoral function, and today it seems to me clearer than ever that all of our sophisticated attempts to find substitutes for it have failed and are doomed to failure. I wish that these personal convictions about the pastoral ministry had been mine from the beginning, and I pass them along with the hope that some young minister will see at the beginning what became clear to me only with longer experience.

Let us be very sure that we are not talking about a man so wise and so well educated that he can give people answers to their problems. If this is the idea of the pastoral ministry, it is a vain one and no one is able to fulfill it. It is amazing to me that a good many people still think that if the pastor cannot advise people on the basis of superior knowledge, he is of no use. They make this same criticism of the preacher who is never wise enough to speak with authority in all the fields of human knowledge and human endeavor. So it is assumed that if there are people in the congregation who are smarter than I am about medicine or the techniques involved in getting us to the moon, then there is nothing for me to say as a Christian spokesman. But if in the common affairs of living and human relationship Christ has given to me some true word, I may assume that the most knowledgeable man in my congregation will need to hear it even as the most humble and uneducated.

In 1604 St. Francis de Sales, a Catholic priest, bishop, preacher, wrote a letter to a young friend and protégé, André Fremyot, newly appointed archbishop of Bourge. He said: "I wish merely to say this one word: a preacher's knowledge is always sufficient when he has no desire to appear to know more than he actually does. Are we unable to speak well on the mystery of the Trinity? Let us say nothing about it. Are we not sufficiently learned to explain St. John's 'inprincipio'? Let us leave it alone. There is no lack of other more useful subjects; there is no question of our doing everything." That is a true word and a good one for us today. Or as John Wycliffe put it in answering the question of how the Word of God must be preached: "Appropriately, simply, directly, and from a devout and sincere heart."*

Now and then a man is tempted to pretend to know more than he does about fields where he is at best a layman. Besides the real danger of being found out, this kind of attitude is really not very helpful to those we come to as pastors. Indeed, it is sometimes very encouraging for people to hear a man who talks so much about living victoriously confess that he does not know the answer to some questions. There was a poor woman one time who went to bring comfort to a neighbor who had lost her husband. She was asked what she said to her, and she replied, "I did not say anything to her. I just

* James McGraw, *Great Evangelical Preachers of Yesterday*, Abingdon, 1961, p. 15.

made her a cup of tea." It may be that the very act of calling and sitting quietly with another person is the best healing we can bring. At least, it has come to me that I do not need to be ashamed of my lack of knowledge if my heart is concerned to help another man find hope.

I remember reading an article about a United States Senator who, it seems to me, was from Idaho. All of this is a little vague, but the main point will be clear enough. He was nominated for a banking commission and the nomination had to be confirmed by the Senate. The report of the examination went something like this: Do you feel that you are qualified to serve on this commission? His answer was yes. Were you a bank officer? No. Were you a board member of a bank? No. Were you ever a bank employee? No. "Then why do you feel yourself qualified to serve on the Banking Commission?" asked the chairman of the committee. The Senator replied, "I was a depositor." The Protestant minister is in a position to answer the questions which may be put to him that he is a family man, a sinner who has been redeemed by Christ, and that he sits where they sit.

In the winter of 1966 it was my privilege to be a visiting professor at Drew Theological Seminary in Madison, New Jersey. My wife and I arrived at the end of a blizzard, and the next day I felt suddenly lonesome and rejected. We were assigned a small apartment, and I did not know anyone around the campus. The three months I was to be teaching there seemed a long, long sentence. In the afternoon there was a knock at the door and a man introduced himself as the minister of the First Methodist Church of Madison. He said he heard of my arrival and had come by to call.

Usually I am rather suspicious if a preacher calls on me, for usually he wants something. But this man did not want anything in the way of an appointment, as he made clear in a little while that he liked the New Jersey Conference and he did not want to come to California—a strange fellow. He had come just to welcome us and tell us that the church was there and anxious to give us any service within its power. Suddenly, my heart was warm and I cannot remember a more enjoyable few minutes visiting with a man who had not come to solicit a subscription to a newspaper, ask me to take milk from his company, or send my dirty clothes to his laundry. And I thought of all those people in our time who are moving to strange places and feel lonely and isolated. Do you not suppose it would make a great deal of difference to them to have a man come from a church to call on them, not to get anything, but to give something? In this mobile age the place of the pastor visiting new families who are far from home is more significant than ever. I knew then that people are not less in need of a pastor than they were in the past but more in need than ever before.

Some time ago I was in the hospital for a day and a night. I was not sick, but having my annual checkup which I do whenever I remember it. In the evening a young preacher from the neighboring Methodist Church came in to see me. He said he had noticed my name on the list of patients as he was making his hospital calls, and he had not heard before that I was ill. I told him I was not sick but that I was glad to see him, and so we visited together for a little while. Then just before he left he said to me, "Bishop, would you like to have a prayer?" I cannot explain what those words meant to me, and I replied immediately, "I sure would." Then he prayed briefly for me and my work, and left. I thought to myself that if I had been sick and the minister had come by and asked to have prayer with me, what an impression it would have made and what an experience it would have been! For when a person is in the hospital facing an uncertain future, how wonderful it is to have a pastor call and pray.

All my ministry I did pastoral work, but I did not enjoy it. As I look back, my greatest difficulty with it was that it did not seem important. As a young minister I could not believe that punching doorbells and stopping by to see folks was worthy of my educational accomplishments. This seemed such a useless waste of my time and energy when I much preferred studying and preparing to preach. Today, however, I know of its importance. I would be a better pastor if I had to do it over again. If by any chance, some young man feels the way I did and can be convinced that there is no place where he will more certainly do the Lord's work than here, it is enough.

Margaret Scherf, who was elected to the Montana Legislature in 1964, wrote of her experiences as a representative of her district in the state government.* These two sentences she wrote stick in my mind: "The national candidates appear at large meetings, dinners, rallies. They make TV appearances, talk strategy with party leaders, shake many hands, but they haven't time to listen for an hour or two to a logger injured in the woods who is unable to collect from the Industrial Accident Board." This is a general situation in our society. The bureaucrats, of whom I am one, have their place in trying to handle responsibility which a church has placed upon them. But so far as persons are concerned, it is the pastor who takes the time to listen to what in the framework of the big strategy of the institution may appear to be minor, but to the person involved is of ultimate significance. By such service is the Church made great and by this ministry do we bring the Lord Christ down.

* *Harper's,* April 1966.

If you have ever fallen into a situation (hopefully not a criminal one) where you need legal counsel and where you are worried about the legal situation, you may have found a lawyer who had not only legal skill but character. In desperation you have turned to him, and he has been able to tell you that he will look after the problem and for you to stop worrying. If you ever saw Perry Mason on TV, you know what I am talking about. This is the position of the minister so often when he calls upon people who are in trouble. He can look at it from an objective point of view and oftentimes help the big thing become small and the unseen issue decisive and real. He is the one who brings comfort and confidence, not in himself, but by his ability to point to the One who loves us and gave himself for us. The doctor whose confidence rubs off on the patient is a pastor in the best sense. So is the plumber or the TV man who can fix what is broken.

There is a tendency for the brilliant man to put himself above the people and thus cut himself off from one of the main sources of his strength. Such a man more than the less brilliant one needs to be a pastor lest he forget what the Christian ministry is and what his service must be.

C. S. Lewis had a very clear insight that applies here when he wrote about Christianity and literature. He said that the unbeliever is always apt to make a kind of religion out of aesthetic experiences. "But the Christian knows from the outset that the salvation of a single soul is more important than the production and preservation of all the epics and tragedies in the world: and as for superiority, he knows that the vulgar since they include most of the poor probably include most of his superiors."* And pastoral work keeps this clear in the minister's mind.

* *Christian Reflections*, edited by Walter Hooper, Eerdmans, 1967, p. 10.

IN THE MODERN SETTING

The man who takes his calling list and starts out each afternoon to stop by homes seems almost like a leftover from another age. They were doing this in my grandfather's day and surely there must be a more efficient way to do it now. Or perhaps it is true that it is no longer relevant. The urban situation certainly is not the same environment in which our fathers worked. Indeed, Professor Cox in his oft-quoted *The Secular City* intimates that people today have come to the city because they prefer anonymity. They have moved out of the small towns because they did not want everyone to know their business. They sought the city where they could have privacy and where they could do as they pleased. This, he intimates, is what they want and this is what they have received.

It needs only to be said that the city pastor does not find it so. In my talks with men serving inner-city churches, they agree that the city is full of lonely people whose loneliness is driving them to despair. The old and the poor may find some attention paid to them by some social agencies, and for this we should be grateful. But what they really need is something the secular social worker is in no position to provide. They ask the same old questions about the nature of life, the nature of death, and the nature of God. The apartment house dweller may be harder to reach and he may have more barriers between him and the pastor, but his need is as great as his father's who lived in a small town. The city is full of loneliness and the pastor need not assume that something or somebody has taken his place in ministering to that terrifying human condition. Riesman wrote *The Lonely Crowd* a few years ago, and that title is the clue we need to follow.

If the need is there, so also is the responsibility of the Church. Any church administrator will bear testimony that the Christian fellowship with no pastoral oversight of its people will not flourish and, indeed, will not hold its own. All the sociological studies in the world cannot provide any substitute for a Christian church doing its work through a Christian pastor and through laymen who themselves have caught the pastoral vision. Certainly we have tried to find some other answer many times.

The great word of our time has been counseling, and a generation of young preachers came upon the scene sure that this was the road for their own satisfaction and for their own service. Indeed, this has been a field to which many turn if they have failed in the work of the ministry. It used to be that a preacher who could not make it became an insurance salesman or found his place in some Christian-social agency like the YMCA. Today, he becomes a counselor, and we have the strange sight of men who have had divorces setting themselves up as marriage counselors to tell other people how to make a success of their marriages.

Dr. Truman Douglas has a word to say about this counseling business and how it actually works out in a church. He writes: "Or, if we were not aesthetically inclined, instead of rearranging chancels we tried our hand at rearranging people's complexes. We put notices in the bulletin stating that at such and such hours we should be available for 'personal counseling.' We were a little astonished that there was no sudden spurt of demand for our services and that when people did come most of them seemed to want us to be just Christian pastors and seldom asked us questions about the emotional consequences of dietary idiosyncracies in children. Since we had just read up on that subject, we had to be content with working it into the next Sunday's sermon."*

This is not to talk against counseling nor to play down the psychological skills we must develop. It is only to insist that this is all fine, but it will never be a substitute for the minister calling in the homes of his people. There is something about a man coming into a family circle and visiting with them warmly about their lives, their problems, and desires, that the professional counselor can never equal. In this part of our work, techniques can never become a substitute for the concerned personality and the loving heart that truly reaches out to people. I have known ministers with very little technical training in this field who were the most successful pastors in the city. Give me a man who will sit down and listen and assure me that he is sincerely interested in me, and I will receive ten times the strength that can come from the one who can only give me a professional psychological analysis.

Now this part of our job is hard work, and that is one reason why we are forever seeking some substitute for it. This is not true for everybody, and there are men who really enjoy this part of the labor and do it easily. I am not one of them, and I can only report what they tell me. For me the hardest part of the ministry was calling, and I was never quite so tired as when I came home after an afternoon of making somewhere around twelve to fifteen calls on my people. It was not enjoyable to me. One of my young preachers who was not doing this part of his work came to see me one day at my invitation. After I told him what seemed to me to be his lack and his weakness, he responded, "But, Bishop, I have a psychological block against calling." My answer to him was, "Son, I have had it all my life—so what?" Others can describe with more enthusiasm the joy of this work while I can only

* *Preaching in the New Reformation*, Harper, 1956, p. 46.

describe the necessity for it and its importance. It is a frightening kind of job, and many a time I have prayed that nobody would be at home so that I could leave a card and run. But today I am sure of its importance.

One of my colleagues described a scene he had observed in Africa years ago when he was on one of his episcopal visits. I think it was in the Congo. He said that in the middle of the jungle they had cleared away the trees and built an airfield. Here were the concrete strips beginning nowhere and going nowhere. A man from the bush would have come to the field, looked at it, and would have said that surely these Europeans were the most foolish people in the world. What point is there in building a road in the midst of the jungle that does not connect villages or towns? If he could have been told, however, that this was really a place to come in to and to take off from, it would have made sense to him. That, said my friend, is what people need so often in the experiences of their lives. Unable to do it on their own, they need somebody to interpret what this seemingly meaningless affair stands for. This is the pastor's job as he helps people to see meanings in the experiences which appear only useless and insignificant.

Christopher Morley wrote one time that this generation seemed to have two main problems. One, the past and how to escape it. Two, the future and how to prevent it. We may have made some great advances in science, but we certainly have not eased the burden of living. Most people are having a hard time, and if the pastor cannot give them solutions, he can certainly listen and it is amazing how often this simple function heals and encourages. Thoreau's announcement that most people live lives of quiet desperation never seemed more true to me than just now.

One of my friends who had drifted away from the church finally came back to it because he had learned how much he needed its influence in reestablishing his life. He wrote to me one day that the night before, the pastor had called on him in his home. He wrote about it as if it were a modern-day miracle and as if something so wonderful had happened that he had to tell me about it. Or, I think of the farmer who came in to visit me from a little town up in the hills, pleading that we should send them a pastor and not just send a student to preach on weekends. "What I need," he told me, "is someone I can talk with about me and life." I knew what he meant, for that is what all people need.

Yet, I can see someone agreeing that this may be all right for some folks, but surely it is not necessary for the great bulk of the fairly successful who are getting along all right. That, my brethren, is where you are quite wrong. In Victorian times the squire and the parson sometimes came into conflict. Professor Owen Chadwick in his book *The Victorian Church** says that the squire of Helmingham in Suffolk would stand up with his watch in his hand when he thought the sermon was too long. But the minister must never assume that the wealthy man or the powerful man stands in any less need of a pastor than the poor and the weak. It sometimes takes more patience to serve them, but their need is not less.

To one of our churches on the edge of the desert a few years ago, I sent a new preacher who began to call on his congregation immediately. In that town there was a very wealthy and important head of a great corporation who lived there for reasons of health. This young man in his calls went to see him because, so far as he was concerned, he was just a

* Oxford, 1966, p. 517.

sinner for whom Christ died and in need of Christian faith as much as anyone else. That very rich and powerful man was so much impressed with this minister calling on him that he joined the church and began to use some of his power and money for Christian causes. No one had called before because they were all afraid of him. I wonder how often this happens.

I am sure that in all communities you will find the "up-and-outers" who are very lonely people. They are cultivated by money raisers who are promoting certain projects. They may never have known a pastor to call and not ask them for something. Believe me, it may come as quite a shock to know that there is somebody in that town who thinks of them only as persons, and that shock treatment may save and redeem them.

In one of the cheap apartments in a city, a woman was found who had been dead several days. She kept a diary, and at the head of each page she had written: "No one called today." It is amazing how little people have changed in all the centuries. When we are talking about this new day and this new condition, we will do well to remember that the pastor's function has not been superseded.

OUR PLACE

The pastor has certain temptations in his work which are very subtle and insidious. He can, if he is not careful, turn into a manipulator of people for some ulterior purpose. A young preacher told me one time that evangelism was just manipulating people. May the good Lord deliver us from the blindness that cannot tell the difference between using people and serving them. Kierkegaard was aware of this tendency on the part of churchmen, and he speaks of the physician needing patients or the teacher needing pupils. So he intimates that some ministers needing congregations may go out and round them up. Against this we must rebel and be careful that we do not fall into the trap of using pastoral work as a salesman who is looking for customers.

It needs to be said that pastoral work is important not only for the people but also for the pastor. For a man to shut himself off from intimate contact with his people is the sure way to diminish his effectiveness in all his other responsibilities. We need the encouragement that comes from meeting the saints who are not known. Even the busy minister who is responsible for a large church ought to have some method of keeping him aware of the places he must visit each week. If you have a secretary as I had in the last church I served, who will remind you that you have not made a decent quota of calls that week, it will be very good for you.

If a man is to be a prophet, then especially he must be a pastor if he is to survive. For the early years of my ministry, I had a great admiration for Ernest Fremont Tittle, pastor of the First Methodist Church of Evanston, Illinois. He was known as a champion of great causes, and he was a liberal preacher always out on the front lines. When he died it seemed clear to me that everybody would remember him primarily as one of the great prophetic voices of his time. I was wrong.

In the summer of 1949 I taught a course at Garrett Biblical Institute in Evanston. Dr. Harold Bosley invited me to fill his pulpit for the four Sundays I was there, and this gave me an opportunity to meet a good number of laymen of the church who had known Dr. Tittle. It was a strange discovery for me to learn that many of them thought of him as a great pastor rather than as a great prophet. One of them told me of the last time he saw Dr. Tittle after his retirement because of a bad heart. He had a call from the pastor one afternoon, asking if he was going to be in and if he could come over and see him. The layman, knowing of Dr. Tittle's sickness, said that he would be in but that he would be glad to come over to the church or to Dr. Tittle's home to see him. But the minister was insistent that since he wanted to ask a favor of this layman, he preferred to come to his home. This man lived on the second floor of an apartment house and there was no elevator. He told me that he remembered seeing Dr. Tittle start up the stairway, two or three steps, and then pause before he could go further. When he finally arrived at this man's apartment, he told him of a mutual friend in the church who was fifty-five years of age and had lost his job. Dr. Tittle had come over to get this man's help in finding him another one.

You may be sure that the prophet who is listened to in spite of opposition and disagreement is practically always a pastor to his people. Some of the men who were most opposed to Dr. Tittle's point of view, defended his right to speak and maintained the tradition of a free pulpit because of their memories of a friend who stood by them when there was death or sickness or failure in their lives.

If you should talk to some of the members of Christ Church Methodist in New York City who have been there for the past years, you will discover that Dr. Ralph Sockman is remembered by them not only as a great preacher but as a fine pastor. This is one side of our work which is so often forgotten or minimized. In all probability you would be hard put to find a great preacher who has not been also a faithful pastor. The two things go together more than we recognize.

The preacher needs the experience for his ministry as much as the people need it for their religious life.

Walter Rauschenbush was the great pioneer of the social gospel in America, and he wrote some of the basic books about the place and theology of that significant movement. No one would have wanted him to take a different road, but he said in the early part of his ministry, "It is now no longer my fond hope to be a learned theologian and write big books; I want to be a pastor, powerful with men, preaching to them Christ as the man in whom their affections and energies can find the satisfaction for which mankind is groaning. And if ever I do become anything but a pastor, you may believe that I have sunk to a lower ideal or that there was a very unmistakable call to duty in that direction." After Bishop Sherrill went to Trinity Church in Boston as a young minister, he says, "My parishioners did more for me that I could ever do for them."

THE ART

There was a great Baptist preacher in Oakland, California, in the days of my youth. He was in my father's church one time speaking before a fellowship dinner, and I never forgot him. Years later, I read his account of three ministers he had known. The first one seemed to say, "Here I am; do all you can for me." Strangely enough, that is what happened in that church, for he was a brilliant person and the congregation was proud of him. They gave him time off for study, money for travel, and seemed to assume that the whole purpose of the church was to carry him around on its shoulders.

The second man seemed to say to his church, "Here I am; let me serve you." They were quite willing to take him at his word, and he became the servant of the congregation. He was an errand-runner and awaited the beck and call of every group in the church who wanted some immediate service. If the ladies were getting ready for a dinner, they did not want to bother the janitor, so they called the minister and he moved the tables for them. If the young people wanted to go somewhere to a meeting, their parents were too busy to take them but the minister would be the chauffeur. Whenever there was a chore to be done, the congregation assumed that the preacher was the one to set to it.

But there was a third minister who came to his church who seemed to say, "Here is Jesus Christ; let us together serve him." And this man, said Dr. John Snape, was the ideal pastor who kept the eyes of the laymen not on him nor on themselves but on Christ. And so each man felt a new call to his own ministry and the Church became involved in the kingdom both within them and beyond them. This is the task of the pastor.

Henry Adams said that a man cannot be a schoolmaster, a priest, or a senator for ten years and be good for anything else. There is a great deal of truth in that observation. The only thing that saves us is to become pastors as well as priests and prophets. For we stand constantly in the danger of what Carlyle defined as speaking with eloquence of a fine purpose and thus making it almost impossible to realize that purpose in our own lives. Keeping close to the people will get us down from our high pulpits and into the life and experience of ordinary men.

It is important that we should be the pastor to all the people. Woe unto us if we single out the rich to be our special pets as one of my colleagues does so cleverly and so disgracefully. I have not been able to make him see why this

approach divides his church and sows dissension in the congregation. We shall have our favorites, no doubt, and a man
has a right to have a few intimate friends with whom he
shares an evening each week for relaxation and pleasure. But
all the people, the likable and the unlikable, the rich and the
poor, the happy and the complaining, belong to our responsibility and service as pastors. The more difficult it is to get
along with a man and the more critical he is, the more we
must pray for grace to see him often and minister to him as if
he were an angel.

I think of a man who has had trouble all his ministerial life
in his churches. Things go well for a year and then suddenly
the church is divided with bitterness and hatred. I have
talked to his people and I have talked to him. My conclusion
is that once anyone speaks a mildly critical word, he writes
him off the list. From that moment on such a man seems to
be his enemy or, at least, no longer his friend. So his life is
one series of enthusiastic beginnings and bitter endings
which finally are brought about by the failure of his pastoral
service to all the people. I will not try to convince anyone
that calling is any fun, but it is one of the things which any
man who becomes a minister must learn to do.

Sherwood Anderson said one time that human beings were
his library. This should not be interpreted as meaning that a
minister may neglect his study or his reading. It should encourage us to see, however, that once we break through the
barriers, every man is of extreme interest and has something
to say that we need to hear. There is a wisdom we do not
acquire in the classroom but only in the face-to-face relationships of the pastor.

Gandhi said one time, "My countrymen are my nearest
neighbors. They have become so helpless, so resourceless, so

inert that I must concentrate myself on serving them. If I could persuade myself that I should find Him in a Himalayan cave, I would proceed there immediately. But I know that I cannot find Him apart from humanity."*

In spite of many disappointments and betrayals the pastor never becomes a cynic. He discovers the greatness of the quiet saints, and he listens to confessions which tell of bravery and courage. Best of all, he learns to know people and to understand the fundamental things about human nature. A colleague of mine one time told me of a very brilliant man who went to Africa and learned half a dozen dialects in a very short time. He was a great linguist and everybody was impressed with his ability to pick up strange tongues. But he was in trouble in a little while and, as my friend commented, he learned the languages but he did not learn the people.

We can easily get overidealistic in our thinking on this subject, however, for there is so much sheer orneriness and pettiness about us that it will take God's grace and power to carry us through. There was a boy one time who never could find a girl who pleased his mother. Whenever he brought a girl he liked, mother always found some reason why she was not the right one for him. Finally, he found a girl who resembled his mother in every way. She looked like her; she walked like her; she talked like her. But when he brought her home, his father did not like her. Sometimes it seems it is about as hard as that to please the people with whom we deal. Pastoral work is never going to be a romantic experience for very long. But we will have enough wonderful and glowing experiences to keep us at it without despair.

The truth the pastor must not forget is that people need

* Quoted by Bernard E. Meland, *The Secularization of Modern Cultures*, Oxford, 1966, p. 6.

some recognition. Ministers forget this because they are in special positions. It is not unusual for them to have their names in the paper, and there are always those faithful saints who will compliment them on anything they do whether it is worthy or not. We forget how many persons there are who receive no recognition for anything they do. One of the best things a good pastor does is write letters to some of his people who have done some service to the church or perhaps have done nothing in particular. A good deal of outstanding pastoral work can be done from one's desk and through a phone call or a letter. If occasionally you would send the president of the Woman's Society some flowers, you would be surprised how much smoother the whole church life will flow.

Churches could do a good deal more than they do in giving awards for special kinds of service. In Hollywood there are many men who have plenty of money and would not be tempted to walk around the block for a sizable honorarium. But they will cross the country and speak for a recognition award for some special service they have performed. We are all like that and we are happy to receive some bit of parchment which we can frame and put on our study wall which isn't worth fifty cents intrinsically. A pastor may have to say some hard words now and then, but he ought to speak a hundred kind words for every critical one.

Years ago I had a friend who was one of the great preachers of England. W. E. Sangster preached to great crowds in the Methodist Central Hall in London. In one of his books he tells about going to preach one evening and stepping up into a doorway to await the passing of a shower. Another man was there and Sangster told him who he was and where he was going and invited this man to come to the service. The invitation was accepted and that night this stranger was soundly converted and gave his heart to Christ. In the years that followed as they came to know each other better, this man would sometimes say to Sangster, "Imagine stepping up out of the rain for a moment and having your life completely changed."

This is the drama and wonder of the pastor's work. When a man leaves a pulpit to go somewhere else and the members of his congregation will be telling him kind things he did for them, he will discover in all probability that they remember some pastoral service. It may be a little discouraging for the preacher to have so few of them refer to a great sermon. But they will remember a call which he has forgotten or a word spoken that made no impression on his memory. Yet, at a particular moment in a particular place, a man with a particular need found a pastor that was used of God to say the right word. It is this pastoral experience that warms a man's heart and makes him realize what a privilege he has had in working with his people.

No other man in the world is expected to be with others in their most solemn moments. Who else baptizes the babies, marries the young people, and buries the dead? What other man is expected to enter the home at a time of great joy and of great sorrow? Who else knows so much about the intimate happenings of so many people? It is the kind of a task to break a man's heart and to drain his strength. But to be a pastor is a privilege and an honor bestowed only on the minister.

On April 26, 1887, the magazine editor, Thomas Bailey Aldrich, rejected a sonnet a lady had sent to him for publication. Among other critical remarks about sonnets in general, he wrote: "Why should we print in a magazine those intimate revelations which we wouldn't dream of confiding to the bosom of an utter stranger at an evening party? In what respect does the stranger differ from the public which we are so ready to take into our innermost confidence?"

Aldrich, however, rejected the poem for the wrong reasons. People are so isolated that they will confide in perfect strangers with the slightest encouragement. God sends pastors to Christian congregations to listen with sympathy and speak with love. And like the Catholic confessional, the Protestant pastor must never betray a confidence. To carry this burden, he must know God and someone who will share it without expecting to know what it is.

IV THE PROPHET

The lion has roared;
who will not fear?
The Lord God has spoken;
who can but prophesy?
—Amos 3:8

Any man dealing with ministers soon learns to put them into one of two main groups. On the one hand, there is the pastoral preacher who deals primarily with personal problems and with individual situations. He is the one people turn to when they are in trouble, and both his word and his presence are comforting and healing. He sees his job as primarily binding up the wounds and comforting the afflicted. His is a noble calling, and probably no man in his community will be loved by so many people and few men will be able to give a better account of their lives.

The second category may be called the prophetic, and these ministers are the prophets. The prophet is devoted to a proclamation of the Word and is aware that the gospel is oftentimes not peace but a sword. He sees the evil and the exploitation of the poor and weak by the strong and rich. He is Amos on Main Street, proclaiming in the name of the Lord the evils of society. If what he says will offend some of the rich members of the church, it is a secondary matter in his mind, for he has been called to proclaim the hard truth and not defend an institution. It is hardly too much to say that in his mind the institution must come second and the Word must always be first.

In the Old Testament the prophet and the priest represented two different callings. The priest was the man of the institution who gave daily attendance to the sacrifices and the worship. He was close to the people through their family relationships and their personal problems. He gave men help in realizing the presence of God by liturgy and symbolism. We must never assume that men do not need that help. At his worst he becomes a religious organization man, demanding the crucifixion of Jesus and the persecution of Paul. At his best he is the Christian pastor.

The Old Testament prophet did not have a settled congregation, and he did not have to worry about such things as meeting the budget of an institution. He gathered his crowd on a street corner and proclaimed his word in the market place. He did not have a very high opinion of accepting responsibility for the household chores of the institution. So, we remember his oftentimes spectacular acts and the burning eloquence of his attack on the established order. Looking back on priests and prophets, we are likely to admire the prophet the most. The contemporary society, however, was more inclined to kill him or drive him into exile and honor the priest.

We have to combine both of these tasks in the Protestant ministry, and it is no easy assignment. We do not have two orders but one here, and the same man should be both a pastor and a prophet. It can be said at once that he will need to be both if he is to do either job in a way pleasing to his Lord. The good pastor has to say things very often which are not comforting, and the prophet had better be sure he knows the burdens being borne by his people. "Comfort, comfort my people" was spoken by a prophet (Isa. 40:1).

The prophet as minister is always in danger of finding a favorite target and attacking it mercilessly week after week. Voltaire, who had a very great horror of being obtuse or ponderous and fled from all bores as if they were the devil, said one time: "My motto is, to the point." This is the prophet's motto as well, but he must make sure that he does not labor the same point so long and so often that people long for a more balanced spiritual ration. There is hardly any other part of our work which is so full of temptation to overstate and narrow down. But woe unto the man who decides the danger is too great and decides to remain an exile from this world of the minister.

One of the most inspiring examples of the church administrator who was at the same time a prophet is related by Walter Russell Bowie.* An Episcopal Bishop of New York said in 1965, "I have learned that a very large gift towards the completion of this great Cathedral was stricken out of one man's will because of the Diocese's stand on Civil Rights. That happened to be in Manhattan. In other parts of the Diocese, this Cathedral which I would like to see completed has lost financial support because of the stands that I as a Bishop of the Church of God have felt compelled to take." Then he added these great words: "If in the providence of God it turns out to be that this unfinished condition is going to prevail for years, then I can only hope that its very unfinished quality will stand as a memorial to a Diocese which in

* See Yourself in the Bible, Harper, 1967, p. 63.

the twentieth century tried to do what it believed was right."
A prophet in a bishop's robes!

THE CONTEMPORARY SITUATION

We must begin with the assumption that most people come
to church looking for help rather than for the truth. The
young preacher is likely to assume that his own passionate
seeking after the reality of the gospel is shared by the people
sitting in his congregation. This, unfortunately, is not true,
and a man must learn to have sympathy for people who are
aware only of their need for help. The deeper thing to have
in mind is that the truth will help us even when it hurts us,
and as our Lord intimated, we cannot be free apart from it.
We must remember, however, that we are dealing with travelers who will assume that they need a helping hand up the
next hill more than the need a revelation of what their journey means. There are some periods which are more antago-
nistic to the prophet than others, no doubt, but in general his
situation is the same. The people do not hear him gladly
unless they know him and trust his sincere concern for
them.

The classic conflict between the prophet and society is
found in the Book of Amos. Amaziah, the priest at Bethel,
complained about the prophesying of Amos to Jeroboam, the
King of Israel. He charged: "Amos has conspired against you
in the midst of the house of Israel; the land is not able to bear
all his words" (Amos 7:10). The common complaint is that
the people are not ready and the land will be hurt by such
bitter and powerful pronouncements. Then the priest says to
the prophet himself: "O seer, go, flee away to the land of
Judah, and eat bread there, and prophesy there; but never

again prophesy at Bethel, for it is the king's sanctuary, and it is a temple of the kingdom" (Amos 7:12-13). There are places, the priest is saying, where this kind of thing can do little harm, and you must go there and speak the words to those people who are not making the decisions. But the reply of the prophet is uncompromising: "I am no prophet, nor a prophet's son; but I am a herdsman, and a dresser of syca-more trees, and the Lord took me from following the flock, the Lord said to me, 'Go, prophesy to my people Israel' " (Amos 7:14-15).

Amos lived in the eighth century B.C., and yet these words could be spoken today and understood so far as the attitudes expressed are concerned. This is the whole problem of the minister being a prophet. Men in our time will tell him that he must prophesy at his own expense, and as long as he is going to take his salary from a church, he must do nothing that will jeopardize its budget or its program. His only safety is to have a church with a great sense of the importance of a free pulpit, or he must carry a majority of his people with him.

This sounds very frightening, but actually most churches have the tradition that a man is not to be dictated to by a committee or a congregation. Preachers have been saying things from their pulpits which their leading members do no agree with for a long, long time. It is possible to be men of conviction and at the same time to be respected. I venture that there is not a minister alive who has not had to speak his truth with love and discovered that his pastoral relationship was not jeopardized.

One of the fundamental questions for the prophet is al-ways: Is a Christian order of society possible? He is concerned with the problems of justice and opportunity. He does not have to be a sentimental man who assumes that men will reach the state where they are capable of ordering their lives according to the rules of Christ. He will not deny that good men are the only hope for a good world. He believes, however, that enough good men are available to influence the half-committed or the uncommitted to the passing of laws which are just. He believes that while legislation is not the way to prepare men for the kingdom of heaven, it is one of the ways by which a nation places a foundation of righteousness under its policies. He believes that minimum standards of decency must be maintained and that those minimums must be constantly enlarged by law.

The criticism of the social gospel and its proponents is only partially justified. There may have been a few who assumed that legislation was the only way to usher in the kingdom. But the majority of the proponents of the social gospel are always aware that they are talking about certain minimum or basic standards which a society may adopt. The preacher who is speaking a prophetic word to his own community is urging a commitment to a framework of justice which is not only possible but is absolutely essential.

Another one of the questions a prophet is concerned with is whether or not the universe is capable of a spiritual interpretation. He is a religious man who believes that God has created the natural order and that human society must be amenable to the divine rule. The significance of this faith becomes clear when we contrast Machiavelli with Amos. For the prophet assumes that any nation or any society is responsible to God and that to deny that responsibility is to court disaster. What God demands of me and society are the questions which the prophet always brings before the people. His is no cynical manipulation of social forces to obtain some definite political end. He speaks out of faith in God and in men as the sons of God.

The great prophetic tradition of the Old Testament tells us how varied were the gifts of the prophet and how various were their approaches. The prophet may be a mystic, or a reformer, or a critic, or a pioneer, or a poet. But always he is an enthusiast. Hegel said that nothing is accomplished without a great passion, and whatever else the prophet may have been, he was a man with a great passion for God's justice among men on this earth. Indeed, he was bound with a sense of obligation which he could not escape and which he could not deny.

Jeremiah is an example of the prophet made captive by God. This sensitive person, who did not want to stir things up or arouse opposition, felt compelled to speak the word which branded him as subversive. Only now do we begin to comprehend his devotion and his faithfulness to his task. Many times he was tempted to flee from the responsibility, but he reveals to us how God takes hold of a man and will not let him go. And so Jeremiah writes:

If I say, "I will not mention him, or speak any more in his name."
there is in my heart as it were a burning fire
shut up in my bones,
and I am weary with holding it in,
and I cannot."
    (20:9)

Here is the prophet's authority and here is the prophet's power. Here also is the prophet's anguish. The congregation comes to feel finally that he is in the grip of something much bigger than himself, and he is proclaiming a word laid upon him by the necessity of God. The man who speaks after this wise may not always be liked, but the respect the people hold for him will carry his influence into all parts of the community's life.

THE MODERN NEED

The more sophisticated our society becomes, the more it is in need of such a ministry. We are probably face to face with more terrible issues than any generation before us has faced. Albert Einstein said, "The world is not ready for it [the atomic bomb]." And then he added, "If I had known that the Germans would not succeed in constructing the atom bomb, I would never have lifted a finger." The great scientist had no illusions as to what he had helped to create.

Said J. Robert Oppenheimer, "In some sort of rude sense which no vulgarity, no humor, no overstatement can quite extinguish, the physicists have known sin; and this is a knowledge which they cannot lose." What a strange thing it is that a scientist should say a thing like that in a day when a vast number of people are saying that the idea of sin is outgrown. I suppose it must mean that Oppenheimer felt there was no other word which would quite express what he and others like him had experienced.

The pilot whose reconnaissance helped choose Hiroshima as the target for the bomb said, "I often see in my dreams women and children running in and out of fires, and it's just hell." The condition of our world may not make the prophet's task any easier, but it certainly makes his task relevant.

Society is always in danger of falling into serious sickness and not recognizing it. Sometimes the worst possible thing is to have no symptoms. We need not be so concerned for a generation that feels that it is facing problems unparalleled.

We would need to feel very concerned for a generation which might assume that all was well and the main problems of human life have been solved. One of the serious situations we face is an assumption that irritation, or neurosis, or discontent, or worry are unnatural conditions of man. On the contrary, these are the things which stimulate man's growth and awaken him to reality.

We need, therefore, someone in every society to proclaim its sickness. Herman Melville described it as the pulpit fulfilling the place in society the prow fills for the ship. From that vantage point the storms and rocks should be discerned and the warning given. What the prophet has done through all the years has been to stay ahead of the majority in discerning the dangers of the future. Oftentimes they will not listen until it is too late, but that does not excuse the minister from assuming the prophet's responsibility. For he may find himself now and again like Jonah being listened to by the Ninevites, and arousing in his people a desire for repentance.

J. H. Plumb, author of *Sir Robert Walpole* comments on how the English statesman obtained and maintained power for a very long time.* He was the wheeler and dealer of England and as artful a politician as England ever knew. Kings lived and died, but he seemed to go on forever and assumed that the job would be his forever. Toward the end, however, friends died and friends deserted him, until the majority saw him no longer as the road into the future but as a dead end. There appeared on the political scene young William Pitt, who made Walpole the chief target of his barbed attack. After his long years of being cast aside and disregarded, Pitt became the voice of the time. And when Plumb compares that time with our time, he speaks of the

* *Saturday Review*, Jan. 28, 1967.

need for a voice like Pitt's now and for a recovery of the power of moral ideas and great language. The great religious leaders who for many years "seemed to unlock the significance and duties of human life" seem to have disappeared or grown weary. Dare we believe that such a time can be recovered and that such a role can be reestablished?

In 1775 William Pitt spoke before the House of Lords and he pleaded for peace with the American colonists. His words ought to be remembered: ". . . Yet, when I consider the whole case as it lies before me, I am not much astonished, I am not surprised, that men who hate liberty should detest those who prize it; or that those who want virtue themselves should endeavor to persecute those who possess it. . . . The whole of your political conduct has been one continued series of weakness, temerity, despotism, ignorance, futility, negligence, and the most notorious servility, incapacity, and corruption. In reconsideration I must allow you one merit, a strict attention to your own interest, in that view you appear sound statesmen and politicians. You well know, if the present measure should prevail, that you must instantly relinquish your places. Such then being your precarious situations, who should wonder that you can put a negative on any measure which must annihilate your power, deprive you of your emoluments, and at once reduce you to the state of significance for which God and nature designed you." Would it not be great if we had some men daring to speak to our time and to our people with that spirit and in those tones?

The recovery of our responsibility to be spokesmen for God to His people is of the greatest importance. When I think of the little, easygoing attitudes we take toward preaching and when I think of the great prophetic voices of the past, both in the pulpit and out of it, I am overwhelmed with shame that our high calling should have fallen so low. Yet in my own lifetime I have known a few such men who in their particular place became the center of hope for the future. Not always did their causes win and not always were their warnings heeded. But they made the pulpit a Mount Sinai, and from it again there came words clothed in a divine authority even when those who heard them sought excuses not to heed them and sought for reasons not to believe them. These are the men who make the pulpit a throne and are rightly regarded as the royalty of the ministry.

CONTROVERSY

Whenever we think of a prophet we think of a fellow who is saying something unpleasant to people who do not want to hear it. He is the man who calls down coals of fire on the heads of exploiters and offends all the well-to-do people in the congregation. He is the man who makes us aware of the poverty at our doorstep and exploitation just around the corner. Being human, most of us would much rather pretend these things do not exist at all, but we cannot pretend if the preacher is giving us the chapter and the verse for his accusations.

Let us not forget that controversy is a part of any life and any situation that is vital. The teachers in a tax-supported school were urged by the principal to avoid all controversial issues. One teacher replied, "But all the vital issues are controversial." Quite so. Say something that everybody will agree with, and you have said something that isn't worth saying.

I remember that some years ago I went to a neighboring city to speak at a service club. The man who introduced me gave a very glowing introduction about some of my activities and then presented me as "a controversial speaker." First I was angry at this introduction because I wondered how he knew what I was going to say, and there have been many times when I spoke on a low key theme. Then I began to think how I would have reacted if he had introduced me as "a noncontroversial speaker." I would have been insulted and angry. I made up my mind that I would not seek to stir up controversy on every occasion as some of the brethren do whom I might name, but that I would certainly try to be known as a man who, when the occasion demanded it, would deal with things which were far from comforting.

Controversy is almost inevitably bound up with the idea of leadership. No man really leads his church and no man leads his community unless he has the courage to march ahead. Eli Lilly, in a history of Christ Church Indianapolis, came to the conclusion that its ups and downs were not the result of external forces at all, but were always due to the quality of the leadership. He concludes with these words: "The thoughtful study of Christ Church history since its establishment shows one outstanding revelation. Leadership is the pearl without price."

Along the same line is the conclusion of Dr. Douglas Horton in which he says, "The older I grow the more clearly I see that leadership is basic. Time and again we have witnessed in a church a change for the better or for worse with the coming of a new minister. . . . Given the same people, the same social environment, the same instruments to work with, one man will discover to the church its real reason for being and uncap latent forces of great spiritual power while the other will fail."*

* "The Idea of a Theological Seminary," *The Hartford Quarterly,* Summer 1963.

In my twenty years of experience as a Bishop of The Methodist Church, I stand amazed at the ecclesiastical miracle one man can perform. Here is a church so sick that there seems to be no hope for it, but a minister with courage and concern will change it almost overnight. It is a mistake to believe that the men who can do this are the weak brethren who raise no issues. They are, on the contrary, the men who make the church understand the dignity of its calling and the relevancy of its witness.

It is the prophet who will restore sanity to a people. In the days of the gladiatorial games in the Roman coliseum, Telemachus sat watching two gladiators trying to kill each other. Unable to stand it, he leaped between them and cried out, "In the name of Christ, forbear." Two swords ran him through, but it spelled the end of such brutal killings for the entertainment of the public. The part the prophet plays in finding the word to describe the sin and hurling forth the demand for Christians to incarnate the new way may restore sanity and may demand a martyr.

People get carried away by the madness of the hour. They are like the old Ozark mountaineer at the county fair who listened to a political speech and shouted himself hoarse. Asked later what he thought of the speech, he replied, "I didn't come here to think. I came here to holler." Society, unfortunately, has more than its share of such people, and it takes the eloquent, blunt power of a prophet to bring the people face to face with the issues and quench the fire of madness.

The prophet is a man who knows the past so well that it can speak to him and through him to the present generation. Such a man knows how much of our vaunted progress is merely a changing of style. We are forever in need of someone to keep us aware of the eternal principles which must undergird our life if we are to tread safely into the unknown. Robert Frost had a good word when he wrote:

> Most of the change we think we see in life
> Is due to truths being in and out of favor.*

Or to say it another way, the prophet is the man aware of the eternal laws of God and the unchanging demands which life puts upon every generation.

THE AUTHORITY OF THE FUTURE

There have been few times when the future loomed before us with such bright promise and such terrifying possibilities. We wish that someone among us could foretell tomorrow, and anybody who claims to have that power is listened to with unseemly attention. But foretelling the future is not an essential part of the preacher's task. As prophet, he must be a constant reminder that men are

> to do justice, and to love kindness,
> and to walk humbly with your God.
> (Mic. 6:8)

The future is in the hands of God, and its shape depends upon our willingness to walk humbly with Him today.

There was a social worker who helped a crippled boy to get healed. She arranged for his operation, and in two and a half years he was walking under his own power. This was a great moment for him and for her. Telling the story later, she

* From "The Black Cottage" from *Complete Poems of Robert Frost*. Copyright 1930, 1939, by Holt, Rinehart and Winston, Inc. Copyright © 1958 by Robert Frost. Copyright © 1967 by Lesley Frost Ballantine. Reprinted by permission of Holt, Rinehart and Winston, Inc.

asked finally, "Where do you think the boy is today?" Some guessed that he might be an engineer, or a doctor, or a lawyer, or a minister, or a congressman. "No," she answered, "he is in the penitentiary at this moment sentenced to death in the electric chair for first degree murder." And then she said, "You see, I was so busy teaching him how to walk that I forgot to teach him where to walk." This defining of goals is the task of the prophet. He is to describe the kind of future we ought to have and the way we must form it. Progress is not automatic and life must be molded and guided.

This is the kind of obligation which demands long hours of study and hard work. Jim Ryun's coach said about the brilliant distance runner, "When the day arrives that he thinks he has arrived, he will be finished. If he doesn't continue to improve, then people are gonna cut him to ribbons, and that's one reason I think it's better for him to give up some of the things college kids do. If he has all the social life that some youngsters have, and if he has all the academic life that some of the others have, and if he's got a girl friend and a car and he is doing all these things that some college kids do—this is fine, but he won't be a champion runner." So the preacher who wants all the luxuries and comforts of life will never speak with the authority of men who are dedicated to the prophetic role of their ministry.

When in the late twenties Gandhi visited England, he held no government position and some of the English papers asked, "On what authority has he come?" Gandhi replied, "I come clothed with authority—the authority of the needs of my people." So the prophet comes with authoritative knowledge of God and men and of acquaintance with the victims of injustice. He comes with the authority of experience and a divine commission.

THE PROPHET'S SPIRIT

It is a mistake, I think, to assume that the prophet has to be a man of a certain temperament. I have known in my day men who were outspoken, brusque, and not very patient. Their words were sharp and clear, and they were regarded with respect but seldom with affection. They played an important part in the church's life, and when they spoke, thoughtful men were willing to listen because they knew they would be given accurate information, objective judgment, and intellectual understanding of the issues. Sometimes these were men who liked to shock people, but those who had the patience to hear them out came to trust them in spite of their gruff surface. Perhaps today we have more than our needful share of these "shockers," and one of the signs that the stain of the world affects the Church is the number of men who would rather make a headline than convert a soul. On a little different basis, they are the pharisees who love to be seen in public places and revel in parading their iconoclasm.

But there are other men whose ministry is prophetic, and they are gentle and kind. These are the men who have earned the love of their people because of their own honesty and sympathy and patience. I think of one of them now and always felt that when we talked together he was half apologetic for raising the issue with me. But as we talked further, I knew that he knew what he was talking about and underneath the surface he was boiling with indignation at some of the things he had observed. After we talked together for a little while, I was never at ease until I joined his cause or had done something for it which he wanted me to do.

An old Scottish preacher walked with a colleague as they

discussed last Sunday's sermons. This can be a very painful experience, and sometimes you hear a rehash of a mediocre discourse which was more than you bargained for. But this man confessed that he had preached on the text, "The Evil Shall Be Cast into Hell." The other man's question was, "Did you preach it with tenderness?" It is a good word for every man whose moral indignation is easily inflamed. For the prophet can so easily become embittered toward men rather than toward their sins.

There are a few general principles which we ought to keep in mind, although their application may find each man in a different way. I do not list these as any sure way to escape criticism and trouble but only as general guides when we are preaching on controversial issues.

1. Let us begin where the people are. We dare not assume knowledge of the issues equal to ours, and as a beginning we need to be educators. I am more convinced now than I used to be that a good deal of our unchristian behavior comes out of sheer ignorance. Each man tends to look upon the world through his own eyes and through his own experience. It is very difficult for us to be sympathetic with conditions we have never observed. The poor will know about poverty and the exploited will know about exploitation. But the man who does not come into firsthand knowledge of these experiences will need to be led to an understanding of them through his imagination. This is the kind of prophetic preaching which is preliminary and which ought to be a continual part of our proclamation.

2. Let us assume that we all have the same concerns. It is hardly ever true that there are a few virtuous people who are called upon to beat the sinners over the head with hard words. There is a great reservoir of decency in most men's

lives, and all we have to do is awaken them to the terrible needs of the world and the terrible results of some policies. This will not always work out to a happy ending, but it is always a place to begin.

3. We should assume the possibility of reasonable agreements between us and approach the subject as if we have faith in the good will of one another. The man who begins by raising a barrier and drawing sharp differences need not be surprised if his relations with his people become acrimonious.

4. Let us be inquirers. None of us knows enough about anything to assume there is no more to learn. If we impress our people as being men who will listen to other testimony, we will find them more willing to listen to us. The prophet must be a learner, and every church ought to have what we used to call an inquirer's class where a minister and laymen can explore problems and issues. But in the message itself, he must give the impression that he is anxious for more light and is willing to listen and learn. For every time for a "thus saith the Lord," there are a hundred times for "let us reason together."

5. Let us be biblical. It is amazing how many people will shy off from hard sociological and economical pronouncements from secularists, but will listen to the same propositions if they come from the Bible and are couched in biblical language. This will be no problem for the prophet. The Bible is full of instances where prophets said more direct and disturbing things than most of us will ever be called upon to enunciate. The man who does not want to hear politics in the pulpit and wants his preacher to use the Bible will discover, hopefully before it is too late, that the Bible has a lot to say about these matters which the comfortable would rather not hear. The Bible is our book of authority.

6. Do not back people into a corner if you can possibly help it. Remember that every man has his pride and is likely to react to a logical cul-de-sac in anger. If we can keep the way open for all of us to come to a meeting place without confession that we are foolish or wrong, it will be a good thing. If we must either fight back or suffer an ignominious defeat, most of us will fight back. When a minister said to me recently that he had proved a man wrong before a committee, I could only say to him that such a victory was the worst defeat a pastor could suffer. Let us leave the way open for taking a fresh look at the subject in the hopes that everybody will find a more Christian solution.

7. We must always be pastors before we can be prophets. It has grown on me with the passing years that if we are to serve the Church, we must combine the offices of prophet and pastor until the people will be hard put to tell where one begins and the other leaves off. I have known scarcely a single instance in the last twenty years, of a prophet disdaining the role of the pastor, who did not get into serious trouble. But I can think of no instance where a man combined these two worlds of his calling, that he did not find success and joy in all his work.

8. Let us learn to respect the differences among our people. It is too easy for the minister to assume that when what seems to him a perfectly obvious scriptural command is flaunted, the reason is stubbornness, pride, and sin. Maybe not. It is amazing how people look at the same issue from different points of view and with perfectly clear conscience go in opposite directions. We must beware of making it black or white or of drawing a line which separates the sheep from the goats. I well remember a friend of mine with whom I had very little agreement regarding social issues and had the

hardest time listening to his blatant paganism (that is the only word for it) without telling him I would not stand it any longer. Then he went abroad one summer, and when he came back and we talked together, I discovered that he had learned a great deal on this trip. Some of the things I had been saying apparently had made some impression, and he had met with people and talked with them in a new way. He had come around to a number of positions which if not exactly similar to what I had been preaching, at least showed that he was listening to voices other than the militarist. The prophet needs patience, and as Shakespeare said somewhere, how poor are all of us without it.

9. We must establish confidence, and this will take a little time. When a man gets into trouble and has to leave a parish because of his position on social issues, I think of other men who say exactly the same thing and do not have to leave their parishes. The conclusion is inescapable that it is not nearly so much what we say as how we say it that wins approval or opposition. If we have not become authoritarian and if we are sincere, it will be amazing the extent to which a minister is expected to be a free man and expected to say the unpopular thing if he believes it necessary. Let the prophet be a gentleman and a man of character and he will find a solid support from the main membership of the church.

10. Above all let us remember that we are not the proponents of a particular program to the exclusion of all else. The man who believes that drinking alcoholic liquor is the worst possible sin and the elimination of it would solve all the problems of society, is a menace to the pulpit. So is the man who thinks that all modern sin is bound up in the race issue. Personally, I believe that both of these issues are terribly significant, and I cannot imagine any congregation being left

without these matters being brought to their attention quite often. But life is so big and human beings are so complex that no two or three issues will contain all sin or virtue. We must, therefore, give the man some relief who will listen to us as we express our own convictions with what grace he can muster, if we do not do it every Sunday. The man who rides a hobby whether it be theological or social does not serve his people adequately. It is so good to have a friendly critic (preferably your wife) who will warn us if we are ringing the changes too much on one theme.

THE PROPHET AND THE CHURCH

The Church being an institution is more slow-moving than many a man would prefer. This is not the first generation to have serious doubts about whether any good thing can be expected from the Church. The insistence of some young men that if they are to deal with the relevant problems, they must leave their church, is not new and it is no more true today than it ever was. On the whole we will find that the people who belong to the churches are more open to the prophet's warning than any other group anywhere.

When Lord Melbourne was prime minister of England, it fell to him to nominate the bishops for the established church. He did not like the job because no matter who he nominated, there were always strong parties who disapproved of it. Some wanted a liberal and some wanted a conservative and some wanted a school man and others wanted a plain man of the people. It became a grievous burden to him and he burst out one time: "Damn it, another bishop dead." Yet, one of the great things about the Church is this inability to please it. It consists of not just one party or one persuasion. The men who serve it come from various walks in life and they have various approaches to their service.

The Church is prevented from being too much the reflection of one point of view and one conviction. We must not expect everyone to take the same attitude toward even the burning issues of the day.

There will always be those like Lord John Russell who, as he sat at home on a Sunday with his wife, remarked, "It conduces much to piety not to go to church sometimes." These are the ones who want nothing like enthusiasm disturbing their even ways. As one of the English statesmen said of the Victorian Age, "I can conceive over-activity and over-zeal on the part of the bishops."

But a church only stays alive because it produces prophets, for the church is a servant and not an end in itself. Time after time the situation seems to be as a friend wrote to Newman in 1835: "Everything humanly speaking seems darkening around the church." But God in His mercy touches some man with a new vision and a new hope and the light is rekindled. So when in 1736 Bishop Butler in his *The Analogy of Religion* reported that Christianity was no longer a subject of inquiry but had been discovered to be fictitious and was only a subject of mirth and ridicule, let us remember that shortly afterward, the Wesleyan revival burst upon England. If we must prophesy, let it not be of the death of the Church but of the strange and wonderful way which God appears in the earthly affairs of men through His apostles and His prophets.

THE PROPHET AND THE LAITY

We are writing a good deal in these days about the ministry of the laity as if it were a new discovery. It is really, of course, expressing something which has always been a part of the gospel. Our talk about the place of the laity seems to be full of contradictions. On the one hand, the young preacher who leaves the ministry usually writes an article for some popular magazine on why he left it. Usually he says he was let down by his church members. He goes to some length to define what these laymen should be and what they should do, and he cries aloud how the congregation failed to fulfill those responsibilities. The enemy seems to be the people, and the young man grown disappointed and discouraged decides to try some other field of endeavor where apparently he expects to find better lay support, unless he finds a place where people are not involved.

It seems rather strange in this situation to have other ministers telling us that we must turn more responsibility and leadership over to the laity and that the only hope of the Church is in our lay members. There seems to be a conflict here somewhere and I expect it is in the very nature of the Christian Church. The laity does have a ministry, but the preacher stands alone in his own responsibility especially when he is a prophet. No committee is going to do this for him, and the congregation will never assume the role of Isaiah, nor will a committee become an Amos.

So a representative of the World Church writes these words: "But since our God has a terrifying sense of humor, once in a while, he calls a man to behave in a very unchurchly way and to become a lonely, superb preacher. He is not in any sense the example on which we all have to model ourselves. He is an extraordinary gift to the church."* What is wrong with a statement such as this? It hardly seems appropriate to connect the creation of a great preacher with God's

* Albert H. Van den Heuvel, *The Humiliation of the Church*, Westminster, 1966, p. 75.

sense of humor, for one thing. Whenever an outstanding person appears of any kind, it does not speak to me about God laughing at us but about God caring for us and blessing us. But one thing is true about this man's point of view, which is that this part of the preacher's job will be lonely.

This may be something we have lost in our time. We have been so anxious to have our ministers fill their role of community leaders and all-round good fellows that the man who surrenders membership in the service club and chairing every neighborhood committee in order to know God better, becomes a very rare fellow. The greatness of the calling fades away in the surrender to social pressure.

One of the best statements expressing this necessary but lost attitude for the minister is from Dr. Floyd Doud Shafer,* He writes: "Fling him into his office, tear the office sign from the door and nail on the sign, study. Take him off the mailing list, lock him up with his books—and get him all kinds of books—and his typewriter and his Bible . . . force him to be the one man in our surfeited communities who knows about God . . . set a time clock on him that would imprison him with thought and writing about God for forty hours a week. Shut his garrulous mouth spouting remarks and stop his tongue always tripping lightly over everything non-essential. Bend his knees to the lonesome valley, and fire him from the PTA and cancel his country club membership. Rip out his telephone, burn his ecclesiastical success sheets, refuse his glad hand, put water in the gas tank of his community buggy and compel him to be a minister of the Word." To which I would only comment that if this is exaggeration, it is exaggeration in the right direction.

An architect one time remarked about Le Corbusier that

* *Christianity Today*, Mar. 27, 1962.

he "seemed in his final works to be invariably on the threshold of some new discovery. No other architect created so much anticipation, even surprise among his admirers." Those words could be written about the prophetic function of the ministry. It is always on the verge of something new and wonderful. The prophet sees God breaking into life at every corner and promising divine surprises at every turn. If he is sometimes attacked as being a dangerous man so far as the status quo is concerned, he is always regarded as one who brings excitement into the Christian's role in society, and he brings resurrection to the dull issues of dead theologians. If the contemporary ministry is to find its lost glory again, it will be the prophet who will restore it. Or as a book reviewer put it in another connection: "Probably it is preaching to the already converted; certainly there are no startling new programs and proposals, and the author would be the first to agree that much of what he is asking for may be unattainable. Yet, even so, there are worse kinds of preaching than to the faithful. Even us True Believers need to be reminded, from time to time, that it is possible to believe the obvious, old-hat things that we do, and still be all steamed up about them."* That, brethren, is the prophet's role and responsibility.

* Eric Larrabee, reviewing *Power in America* by David Bazelon, *Harper's*, May 1967.

V THE THEOLOGIAN

> . . . that is, God was in Christ reconciling
> the world to himself, not counting their
> trespasses against them, and entrusting
> to us the message of reconciliation.
>
> —2 Corinthians 5:19

It was reported in a recent magazine that one of the most admired young Mexican writers is José Augustin, who wrote his autobiography at age twenty-two. The report went on to suggest that presumably he will be adding postscripts to later editions. It is especially characteristic of our time for young people to assume that they have learned everything worth knowing already and whatever comes from the older folks is to be dismissed contemptuously. This is always more or less characteristic of youth, and all of us who are now older will remember having gone through these periods when we believed and said essentially the same thing.

When the University of California students were in revolt a while back, they concocted the slogan "Do not trust anyone over thirty." So the new generation discounts the old and believes that all wisdom was born with it. It takes a dim view of tradition and history. It is probably true that some genera-

tions revolt against history more than others, but we are not
to assume that this is in itself something radically new or
different.

Yet, when I look back over my own life and remember the
things I said at the beginning of my ministry, I am utterly
ashamed. It is a revelation of how much the Church can stand
and how tough it is to endure all the nonsense it has listened
to from young preachers fresh out of theological schools.
There was a time at a young people's camp when I was the
reigning radical because I announced with assurance that the
doctrine of immortality was probably false, but that in any
case it was irrelevant. Life, it seemed to me, could be mean-
ingful and essentially Christian without bothering with the
question of life after death. If it were possible I would gladly
eliminate this chapter from my life, and if it were to be lived
over, my prayer would be for humility and silence.

One of my friends who had been pastor of a large Methodist Church for many years underwent a very serious operation
for cancer a few years ago. When it was over, he was assured
they had eliminated the whole danger, and after his recovery
he told me the disease had been checked in time and he
would have many years of ministry ahead. A little more than
a year later, they found some very disturbing symptoms and
he went back to New York for another operation. When it
was over, it was clear the cancer had not been stopped and my
friend could not expect to live very long.

I called him up to say some word of comfort and help.
When he answered the telephone, I was struck dumb and all
I could think of was the puerile remark, "Carl, how are you?"
Without any indication of distress, he replied positively and
cheerily, "Why, I'm all right. I have been in this place for
more than twenty years trying to tell people about living and
now the Lord has arranged it so that I shall be able to show

them something about dying. I am all right and how are you?" There I was, having failed to bring a word of hope and faith to my friend, and he had given me a renewing word. How many times this happens to the minister as he seeks to serve his people!

As Easter approached, this friend wanted me to preach for him, as he was sure he would not be able to do it himself. I flew a long way to be with him on that Easter day and found that he had gone back to the hospital on Good Friday and could not be in the service. I preached the best I could that Sunday morning about eternal life and then went to see him before I left the next day. That was the last time I saw him alive, as he died a few weeks later. And so when I read some of the theological bombast and nonsense which is being produced by some of our theologians today, I remember this experience and it seems to me more basic and more authoritative than any of the books which are making such an impression on this generation. It came to me that theology, which is really what we think and believe about God, has its real roots in life and experience and that in the most serious sense, the preacher must be a theologian.

The spirit today, no doubt influenced by press and publicity agents, seems to encourage our claiming more than we know, and stating more than is true. Humility is curiously lacking among us. The Church resembles Harvard University described by President Lowell as a center of learning because the freshman brought so much wisdom in and the seniors took so little out. Let us be grateful for the theologians who are not the victims of this spirit. Let us be less impressed with the ones who are.

A rough rule for the minister is that if a theology cannot be preached, it is really not much good. The preaching has to be centered in the good news. If the doctrine being promoted has no relationship to this concept, it is probably best to forget it. This does not mean that everything in our theological approach has to be optimistic, for G.K. Chesterton insisted that the gospel was partly the good news of original sin. But it must be good news in the larger sense, and it must have some word to speak to men who are not in the cloister but in the market place.

Somebody has remarked that military strategy is too important to leave to the generals. Any activity that has broad human significance can be stultified and smothered by the professionals. When a man makes a living out of a pursuit, he is in great danger of making that pursuit understandable only to a special group of experts. This is why a special jargon is likely to be developed which the ordinary man cannot understand, and only the specially trained men can talk and think about it. This is certainly too often the case with theology.

There is much to be said for the professional in any field, and we ought to be professionals in the sense of being competent and efficient. But there is also a great danger in the decline of the amateur which may be a prevailing weakness of our time. If we define the amateur as a man who does a thing not for money but just because he enjoys it, we will be close enough to seeing the difference between his work and the man who makes his living from it. The amateur explores a field or develops a skill as a part of his relaxation and pleasure. He does it because it is fun, and this spirit oftentimes leads to truth which escapes us when we get too serious. The amateur does not have to be ashamed of lack of originality, for the whole field to him is so wonderful and exciting that whether someone else made the discovery before him has little significance.

Frankly, I am bored to death with much of the modern theology and especially that associated with "the death of God" talk. For there is so much of it that it is very much like the fairy story told by Hans Christian Andersen about the king's new clothes. You remember, the king was supposed to be dressed in wonderful gossamer material that was different from the ordinary stuff that ordinary people had to wear. Whenever he appeared there was admiration from the crowds, until a child said simply, "He is naked." And so it is with some of the high-flown verbiage which is trying to frighten plain men into believing that deep theological thought is beyond their comprehension. The truth is, I suspect, that much of it is, on the contrary, something full of sound and fury and signifying nothing.

In Moscow at Eastertime in 1966 it was reported that mobs tried to break up the cathedral services by shouting, "God is dead." In America *Time* magazine had on its cover the same words with a question mark: "Is God Dead?" When these two things came to my attention, I remembered a French political scientist who said that he was not so much worried about the differences between the two giants, Russia and America, as he was worried about their similarities. This lack of faith is not confined to an out-and-out atheism but is present in the more insidious and dangerous kind of practical atheism which exists within a society which still politely acknowledges God. Whose fault is this? No one's and everybody's. It does seem clear to me, however, that we are not going to be healed by the jargon of professional theology, and it seems much more likely to me that the recovery of faith must always come through the ministers of the Church rather than through an intellectual hierarchy.

It must not be supposed that I favor a general attack on

theology as a discipline. Indeed, I would go so far as to say that some of my best friends are theologians and their role within the life of the Church is a very significant one. The professional theologian must keep us from logical contradictions. He must explore the deeper implications of the simple New Testament words. He must give us historical perspective, and it would be wrong for us to seek any minimizing of his contributions.

Freedom is the word of our time which has become almost a shibboleth. In its name we become apologetic about convictions. We are bludgeoned into a silent acceptance of teaching which denies all we stand for and believe. We are expected not only to allow but to support subversive ideas and actions which if triumphant will destroy the Church. Whatever happened to the idea that a minister is a defender of the faith?

I preached at a college chapel in the East some time ago, and the night before the service the college chaplain invited me to his home for dinner. As we talked together he told me he had concluded that Christianity had nothing unique to contribute, and he was more and more convinced that ours was a losing cause. I told him that it seemed to me that he had a perfect right to hold to that opinion but that he was in the wrong field and ought to be teaching comparative religions. For a college chaplain who is supposed to minister to the students' religious life as a Christian, to believe he has nothing unique to proclaim, seemed to me at best an anomaly and a mistake. Yet, he said this from time to time in various places, and no one seemed to assume that the college founded on Christian principles and supported by Christian churches had any right to question the wisdom of such a man being in such a place. Surely, the Christian faith is more than an easygoing acquiescence of everything without standards or demands. Was there not One who described it as a narrow gate and a hard way?

THE MINISTER AS THEOLOGIAN

But is the minister supposed to be a theologian? Indeed, can he be one? We must recognize at the beginning that our calling prevents us from becoming specialized scholars in any field or final authorities in any part of the intellectual world. This is one of the decisions a man has to make in becoming a minister, and for some of us it was never easy. Most young ministers start out with a great respect for scholarship, and woe be unto him who loses it. But the many demands of the ministerial task will make it practically impossible for him to be a professional theologian. This should not encourage him to be ignorant of the field, nor should it excuse him from reading and digesting as best he can the hard theological thought of the professors. The American church is not likely to give us time or leisure for scholarship which is an end in itself.

As a young preacher I thought the day would arrive when my theology would be settled and secure. It seemed to me very reasonable to believe that a man who is giving full time to the Christian ministry ought to expect certainty in his thoughts about God and Christ. I had my doubts and torments, but it always seemed to me that my father must have passed beyond that tormenting state to assurance.

Now that I am older, such a point of view seems very naïve and ridiculous. There are so many things not clear to me and so many doctrines go far beyond my ability to grasp all their implications. The fundamentalist who can proclaim not only the exact meaning of a doctrine but the exact way it must be put, leaves me far behind. At the end of the day I am more impressed with the mystery of the Christian revelation than I am with my ability to describe it precisely. As a professor put it one time: "Faith without doubt is dead." Whether this is the way it ought to be and whether this is the way God wants it to be, I am not in a position to proclaim with certainty. But when I observe what dogmatism does to the brethren who are afraid to express a question or a doubt, my conclusion is that their way is filled with more temptations to pride than mine.

This does not mean that as ministers we are to have the kind of wide open mind in which nothing lodges or materializes. After these years of my ministry, there are some great convictions which I hold to and believe with all my life. The main one can be summed up in the simple, and to many people, shallow, statement that Jesus was right. In his life and teaching there is a revelation of the main truth about God and about life and about human nature. I find in him the revelation for the necessary truth men must know. To put it in another way, my experience tells me that whenever I move toward him, I move toward the light, and whenever I move away from him, I go toward darkness. This is the central affirmation of my creed and my faith.

Archbishop Nathan Söderblom of Sweden was one of the thoughtful men of his church and a fine scholar. In 1919 in an article in the German theological journal, *Theoligische Literaturzeitung,* describing a turning point in his life, he wrote: "I personally needed a new insight that came to me in the old library at Uppsala one evening about thirty years ago. I did not understand it at all. But the kingdom of God and the activity of God were in the center. The whole room brightened up where I was sitting, and joy came over me. It was not a book that we had to lean upon, but God through Christ had founded His kingdom. The Bible too had its source in God's work. Christianity was no longer a book religion, it was an historical revelation, fulfilled in Christ. With the conception of the kingdom of God the teaching of Jesus was made central, together with his demands. The Sermon on the Mount was not simply an introduction to the temple, it belonged to the holiest of all just like the cross. Christ became no longer to me the sweet savior, but a man of authority and power. Christianity was something that came with moral strength and ethical seriousness. I learned of the firm basis of God's work in the midst of history and some of my inward and mystic piety was pressed pretty hard. Since then I have learned a new kind of inwardness where the hard steel of idealism strikes first." While my experience was not an exact replica of this it was near enough to make me understand what the archbishop was saying. This conviction has been a general and growing one rather than a precise and dramatic revelation. But the formation of a foundation upon which I can stand with assurance has taken place.

Theology as a particular discipline is a sailing ship which tacks back and forth across the main line with the wind. It is always to some extent a reflection of the spirit of the time, and that spirit is notoriously undependable in the long run. It can never sail a perfectly straight course, for the varying winds and tides of a generation's life affect it profoundly. If a man finds his own theological position out of harmony with the prevailing style, let him not panic or even get excited. Let him stand firm enough and sooner or later, he will discover the prevailing thought coming back his way again. In this, theology is like women's fashions, and much of it like the length of the skirt will go up and down with tiresome regularity. Only Jesus Christ is the eternal figure that is the same yesterday, today, and forever. Our understanding of him and our interpretation of him, however, are things which must always betray a contemporary point of view.

In my own comparatively short lifetime, I have watched this process at work. As a student at the theological seminary in the early thirties, the patron saint of the progressive and forward-looking Christian thinkers was Henry Nelson Wieman. His was a kind of refined naturalism which assumed that the scientific method was the only authentic method and that all truth including religious truth had to be discovered and tested by this single mode. In those days I was trying to preach on Sundays, and in a little while this proposition revealed itself as false. It was impossible to proclaim great truths which the Christian faith holds at the center of his life and say that the preacher must follow the scientific method in announcing them and presenting them. Faith never did and never can limit itself to the procedure of science. Still, this was in the air and a man had to be fashionable, and so we all did the best we could. Within that same environment we were being urged to forget the theological obscurity of St. Paul and get back to the simple teachings of Jesus. It took me a little longer to see through the hollowness of this pretense. But, again, along with my compatriots I did the best I could.

The day arrived when this became old hat and there was a new spirit in the air. It struck me with some force in an eastern theological seminary, and it grew out of a conflict between Karl Barth on one hand and liberalism on the other. Barth was all the rage in Europe and on the East Coast, but he had not reached the West Coast seriously or widely in my student days. But out of this confrontation was born neo-orthodoxy, and that hit me with considerable force. For a time it was sheer pleasure to proclaim the paradoxes of Kierkegaard and say things which the simple, Bible-loving Christians were not so much offended by as puzzled. Each one of these movements was a reaction against the previous point of view which had gone too far. It was the sailing ship tacking in the wind.

In the beginning of my ministry it was assumed by many authorities that what we had to do was find what Jesus really said and actually did. The time came a little later when it was just as enthusiastically proclaimed that we could never gain such historical knowledge, and we had better give up the vain illusion that we could. Then we talked about the Christ of faith over against the Jesus of history. In some circles the historical significance of the gospel almost completely disappeared, and we began to put our emphasis on the Christ who was primarily a legitimate object of theology rather than of historical study. Now I notice with great appreciation that there is a swing back toward history and Jesus. It ought not to be necessary to have to go back to something which is central to the gospel. For when we lose the sense of a particular man, in a particular place, at a particular time, being a revelation of God, we have lost the central clue of our religion. The scandal of particularity frightens the learned men, especially the philosophers. And every now and again they manage to infect the theologians with that fear to the detriment of Christian revelation.

Anyone who thinks back a few years will have similar experiences and, hopefully, it will help him to take less seriously the latest theological fad. What society labels as new is usually some neglected truth which has proved to be essential for its life. There is no discipline more exposed to the pressure of fadists than Christian theology.

As a young man I was enthralled by G. K. Chesterton's writings. His discussion of Christian theology which he called *Orthodoxy* was an old book when I first read it (published in 1908) thirty years ago. Not long ago I saw it again and began to leaf through it, and I was captured afresh by its keen perception and dramatic way of stating old truths. It came to me that real progress in this field is an illusion. Our minds are not big enough for the Galilean, and when we get carried away with a part of the truth, the next generation has to bring out the part we overlooked. We call this advance, but it is really recovery of the neglected and a reestablishing of the balance.

THE PRESENT

When we survey the contemporary scene, we are reminded of the New Testament warning that a man's foes shall be those of his own household. The criticism of Christian theology does not come so much from the outside as from the inside. While this attack does not last and soon grows boring, it does prevent the Church from proclaiming the great saving word to a fragmented society rushing around in circles but getting closer to the edge of the abyss with every passing year. Nor can we truly estimate how many young lives have been turned aside from His way by it. A mother told me one day that her high school son, headed for the ministry much to her delight, had turned away from it in doubt and uncertainty when he had read some of the "death of God" theologians. He would not have been so upset, she thought, if the attack had come from atheists outside the Church. But when men who called themselves Christian thinkers made the proclamation, he felt that the whole enterprise had been swept away.

The Church does not need to be concerned about the honest-to-God atheists, but may the good Lord deliver it from the so-called intellectuals who are out trying to make the head-line.

These men are oftentimes philosophers who do not know enough real Christian theology to put in your eye. There seems to be some unwritten law that the Church must never tell such men to go somewhere else, for that would be tres-passing in a forbidden land labeled "academic freedom." Sometimes I wonder if this same problem affects medical schools and if they would feel it necessary to keep a Christian Scientist on the faculty who announced blatantly that he did not believe that sickness is real. Does the same problem affect a law school? And would it be under attack if one of the professors was an anabaptist who thought all law was evil and proclaimed anarchy as the right way? However that may be in other places, so far as the Protestant theological school is concerned, it seems as if anything and everything goes. The man on a faculty of a church college can be sure that he will be a hero if the church raises any question about his teaching pronouncements which destroy its reason for existence. It is time for the Church, either of the liberal persuasion or the more orthodox one, to suggest two or three things. (1) If a man is seriously trying to talk about Christianity and deny the reality of God, he must be too mixed up to be a teacher of anything anywhere. It seems to me fairly obvious if one reads his Bible that the Christian faith has no meaning apart from God, and our Lord rooted all his teaching in that funda-mental affirmation. (2) If some of the new and radical breth-ren do not mean what they seem to be saying, then should they not be sent back to college and take what we used to call in my day "bone-head English"? This was a course which students had to take if they could not write a simple sentence and did not understand the meaning of simple words. (3) If these brethren are tired of being anonymous professors and want to have a story in *Time* or *Newsweek,* we shall understand that, but surely we have a right to suggest that they shall not do this at the expense of the Church and its theology. (4) If the defense is made that really this is all a matter of semantics, then let us proclaim boldly that theology is too important to be regarded merely as a semantic game and such scholars had better find something less serious to engage their attention.

A Church of England bishop wrote a best seller called *Honest to God.* I read it with expectancy to see what new revelation was awaiting me. I came to the end of it feeling that I had heard this stuff all my life and that if there was anything new or fresh about it, to save my soul I could not tell what it was. The only conclusion possible seemed to me to be that this man had a good press agent and that the secular press thought that a radical bishop would be good copy. They did the same thing some years ago with the Dean of St. Paul's Cathedral when they pinned the label of "Red Dean" upon him. Perhaps the real news in this book is that here is a bishop being honest, and I will confess that one might make something out of this if he tried. The whole episode seems to proclaim just one simple thing: this is a theologically illiterate generation. The books, movements, and schools so radical to this generation would have been dismissed in a hurry by the Puritans who sat through two-hour sermons on theological questions.

This, however, should give us very little comfort, for it is simply a reflection of the inadequacy of our ministry. We have kept theological matters to ourselves, and as one professor told me one time, we take such good care of our weak sisters that sometimes and in some places they are all we have left. This whole business should be a judgment on the ministry and its failure to be theological. It is a clear revelation that if we are not theologians, we are not doing our job. We are simply making it easy for the kind of man who hires his own public relations agent to upset a church and lead the people astray.

Our time is characterized by an inordinate desire for that which is new or sounds new. We are like the Athenians of whom it is written in the Book of Acts: "Now all the Athenians and the foreigners who lived there spent their time in nothing except telling or hearing something new" (Acts 17:21). Said Dean Robert E. Fitch in an article in the Autumn 1966 *Religion in Life:* "The Protestant sickness derives in part from a myopia of the mind. With its inordinate passion for Christian novelty, it might do well to take another look at profane antiquity." A contemporary weekly journal of Christian interpretation ran a series of articles some time ago by prominent religious thinkers on how their minds have changed during the past few years. The next step as some wit has put it will be for a magazine to publish a series of articles on "How my mind has changed in the last five minutes," and that will make it difficult for a journal to keep up with the trend. How will we get the magazine distributed before the next new idea comes along? There is virtue in this, of course, and we ought to keep up with the times. There is promise in the Christian theologian trying to make relevant to his present day the old, old story. But when the thing becomes a fever as it has with us, it is a sign not of health but of sickness.

Whatever happened to those old, solid, dusty volumes of theology that were on the shelves of the seminary library? Whatever happened to the theological professor who felt that you were not in any position to judge the new until you knew the old? What became of the assumption that theology did not begin with us and that doctrines will sound new and radical only to people who have never studied the history of Christian thought?

Well, this too will pass in good time. An old professor met me on the campus of Drew University one day and asked me what I thought of this new theology. He said that in his judgment it was all taken care of back at the beginning of the 14th Psalm:

> The fool says in his heart,
> "There is no God."

PREACHING AND THEOLOGY

All of this I have been writing will sound suspiciously like a diatribe, and it must now be said that it is only the introduction to a plea for theological preaching. Our modern sermons have been either so obscure that plain men could not tell whether they were theological or not because they did not listen; or else they have been so lacking in any theological foundation that they are a disgrace to our profession. So many of the sermons I read are psychological or sociological but hardly the least bit theological. That is, they deal with things of the mind and with the things of society but with no roots in the Bible's account of the way God deals with men and nations.

We have had too much of the dominant American philosophy of success hung onto a religious framework with a few pious phrases woven through it. On my way to a preaching appointment one Sunday morning, I tuned in on the radio (never to be recommended) and heard a fellow holding forth in the name of Christ. He was receiving his salary from a Christian church and he was an accredited member of a Protestant communion. As I listened to his sermon that morning, I told my wife that he was no more than a sales manager giving a sales pitch to his salesmen. There has been too much of this kind of empty talking which goes under the name of preaching. You may recall a remark made by a magazine editor some years ago, who read the *Reader's Digest* for the first time. "It sounds," said he, "as if it were written by some damn preacher." He was bearing witness to the popular idea that a preacher deals with some inspirational stuff and tells some stories full of human interest, and that is about it.

We have been afraid that the church is too solemn a place and so it must be made more frivolous. In one of the Beecher Lectures at Yale, George Wharton Pepper referred to Billy Sunday saying to a student audience, "Cheer up! You are not in church." Well, the church ought to be a cheerful place but it ought not to be merely a platform for a man to distribute a little pious advice about how to win friends and influence people.

Great preaching is always theological. An Englishman put it very well when he commented on one of Bishop Matthew Simpson's sermons in these words: "Ah, sir, that was preaching. What a backbone of hard stout thinking was behind all that tenderness and unction." It is a sad and disturbing thought to me that if our laymen are to receive any theology whatever, they are going to get it from the sermon of their minister. A prominent Jewish lawyer told me one time that he would have become a Christian at least two years before he finally was converted, if he could have found a Christian church to tell him what Christianity was really all about. And if the preacher will insist that he is not responsible for this part of the work and that it belongs to the professional, then let us say to him gently but firmly that he cannot pass this part of his task along to anyone else.

The theologian as such is always dealing with secondary material. When he does his necessary work, he needs to realize that this is what he must do. The seminary student tends to read many books about the Bible, and in the press of his obligations he may forget to read the Book itself. There was such a student who, after leaving seminary, read the Bible and commented: "The Bible sure sheds light on those commentaries." It is my belief that the Christian minister is dealing with primary material more than the academic man can ever do.

If this sounds like an exaggerated claim, consider these words of the late H. Richard Niebuhr written as a part of the "How I Am Making up My Mind" series in *The Christian Century*. Said this noted theologian: "Among the facts and reflections most important to me at the present is the fact, recently rediscovered, that theology is a secondary rather than a primary form of discourse. Creeds, sermons, prayers, catechetical literature, are examples of primary discourse in Christian faith. Theology is a secondary form of discourse, having as its purpose reflection upon, appraisal, criticism, and defense of these primary words. . . . I have come to believe that theology is a mode of reflection and discourse continually invigorated, to be sure, by the human passion to criticize and assess but also dependent upon a primary mode of religious utterance. This primary mode, which comes into our view as prayer, psalm, parable, homily, hymn, etc., demonstrates the inner penetration of the political and the familial, the aesthetic and the moral interests of man with his religious interests." This seems to me a most important observation and one we overlook too easily. In the beginning was the experience not the theology.

The dean of one of our theological seminaries has complained that only professors, and they in decreasing numbers, are employed with an explicit mandate to think. He felt that this was a very sad state of affairs, and in a sense it is. Yet, the Church has never employed men just for this one activity. I doubt very much that a group of men chosen by the Church to withdraw to the ivory tower for the sole purpose of thinking about the great issues of our life would serve it with as much effectiveness as the dean assumes. Consider the history of the Christian Church and the men whose writings have shaped its thought.

The place to begin is with the life and writings of the Apostle Paul. There are some who regard him as a theologian, and certainly it is true that there is hardly a single Christian doctrine that cannot find its roots in the Letters of Paul. He seems to have had such a full and complete grasp of the meaning of Christ and the implications of his life, death, and resurrection that I cannot think of a single primary doctrine that does not begin with him. Indeed, it would scarcely be going too far to say that if you cannot find it in Paul, it is not worth searching for. We talk of miracles in the New Testament and what our attitude toward them should be. There is, however, this miracle of the Apostle who never started out to write theology as such but to deal with the practical problems of those early churches in a series of letters which he had written in the midst of a very busy life. Yet we find in those letters the great questions raised and the great affirmations made which have given the Church its theological framework for nineteen hundred years. Is this not a miracle?

The truth is that St. Paul is not a theologian but a missionary. He was a very practical administrator of the early church and involved in the monotonous, disillusioning, petty problems of the various congregations spread across that ancient world. He was a pioneer dealing with men and women who were new Christians coming into its fellowship trailing the clouds of pagan belief which had surrounded them and from which they had just recently made their departure. He was a traveler putting to shame all travelers and setting the style for all the great missionaries of the future. When we think of the primitive modes of travel in his day, his long journeys discredit all the boasting of those of us today who would like to claim credit for being great circuit riders. Certainly, there was nothing merely academic about this man who was the greatest of the theologians.

Or we may consider St. Augustine who in the fifth century set forth the propositions that undergirded the medieval church and profoundly affected it for a thousand years. He was a bishop, and whatever else we may think of bishops, we surely will not regard them as men granted leisure to withdraw from the ongoing life of the churches to think and write. He did not want to be a bishop particularly and would have chosen another road if the people had not risen up and practically forced his acceptance of the office. His work was not only preaching but teaching, and in addition he had to be a judge over the conflicts of the Christians within his bishopric. There is at least one instance where he had to spend time finding a husband for an orphaned girl, which gives us an idea of the kind of activities he was called upon to undertake. The bishop taught the new converts, and this is the man who became one of the great theologians of the Christian Church.

Martin Luther was the father of the Reformation, and his writings have profoundly influenced it until this day. Yet, in his own time he was as much caught up in the conflicts of the day as is Martin Luther King in our time. There was precious little that was academic in Martin Luther's career, and his theology comes red hot out of the fires of conflict and danger.

Let me say a word about John Wesley, who is not regarded by most people as a theologian. However, in recent days we are beginning to see him as more of a doctrinal thinker than some had thought. He wrestled with theology, and he tried to make clear the implications of his belief that experience was at the root of the Christian emphasis. In his collected *Works* it is amazing how much time he spends writing about theological matters and laboring with points of doctrine. All of this, mind you, from a man who in his fifty years of ministry traveled some 250,000 miles on horseback over the rough and dangerous roads of Great Britain.

The theologian of the social gospel was Walter Rauschenbush, who nevertheless regarded the pastorate as the highest calling. Or if we turn to Karl Barth, we hear him tell us that he first began to wrestle with these great issues when as the minister of a church and preparing his sermons, he heard the sound of the guns of war in the distance. Much later on, he preached a series of sermons to the prisoners in the Basle jail, and he never lost his sense of mission to such people. All of these were men whose theology which so profoundly affected the Church came out of the action and the busy routine of pastoral relationships.

Now this has scriptural foundation. The Fourth Gospel

says: "My teaching is not mine, but his who sent me; if any man's will is to do his will, he shall know whether the teaching is from God or whether I am speaking on my own authority" (John 7:16-17). This seems to be an affirmation that knowing God's will is not a matter of contemplation but a matter of action and commitment of life. Whenever we begin to think of theologians as primarily men who are to stand apart from the life of the Church, we are in trouble. William Lewis, writing in a seminary magazine* in 1965, refers to the coming of the sabbath "and that joyous occasion when theologians have to make an attempt to be understood." Indeed, the ecumenical movement could say, echoing St. Paul, that professional academic theologians, very often from Europe, have done me much harm.

THE MINISTER'S RESPONSIBILITY

Theology has always been responsible for saving the Church from heresy, and while that seems like an old-fashioned idea in our time, it is still the theological task no matter how we may word it. The Nicene Creed according to St. Athanasius was a notice board set up to preserve Christian thinking from the heresies threatening the Church. If this was a legitimate task in those days, it is a legitimate task in ours. We are ever in need, as John Baillie one time put it, of going back to the original foundations and cutting through the dogmas which have grown up and become popular. We need to find and face the primary insights, and this is where the minister comes into the terrifying responsibility which is primarily his.

Heinrich Ott deals with our situation in these words: "It

* *The Drew Gateway.*

perhaps must be said that theology is the conscience of the sermon, and in turn that the sermon is the conscience of theology. If he is to preach correctly, the preacher must reflect theologically. And to be able to teach theology, even though he does not himself have to enter the pulpit Sunday by Sunday, the theologian must understand the intention of proclamation and keep the task of the preacher steadily in view. The preacher who does not wish to do so, and hands over the task of theological reflection to the theological 'expert,' is a poor preacher, a preacher without 'conscience.' And the theologian who does not wish to do so, and hands over concern for the proclamation of the church to the 'practitioner,' is a poor teacher of the church, and also a theologian without 'conscience.' "*

Reinhold Niebuhr sometimes argued for a doctrine by showing what would happen if it were denied. Some of the scholars have attacked him for this, but I believe it is a proper thing for a theologian to be concerned about and it is a part of our task. We may argue about the doctrine of the Trinity, for example, and it has become popular in our time to dismiss it or to deny it. In at least one of the churches this is a hot issue in relation to one of its bishops. For me the answer is to be found by following Reinhold Niebuhr's principle: what happens if we deny the doctrine of the Trinity which is in reality a statement of checks and balances to keep our ideas of God and Jesus Christ from flying apart? All we need to do is to look at the Unitarians and see what happens when the Trinity is rejected. I have no new understanding of this doctrine to proclaim, and it has been a mystery and a debate from the beginning. But it has kept the Church from

* Robert C. Johnson, "Who is Heinrich Ott?" in *New Theology No. 1,* edited by Martin E. Marty and Dean G. Peerman, Macmillan, 1964, p. 41.

running off on a side path and getting lost in the bogs of humanism. To me, at least, the chief argument for the validity and the importance of the doctrine of the Trinity is to observe what happens when it is denied.

The minister has to be careful that he does not oversimplify in order to make plain. Said Kierkegaard: "According to the New Testament, Christianity is the deepest wound that can be inflicted upon man and now the modern clergyman is trained in the art of introducing Christianity in such a way that it signifies nothing, and when he is perfect in that he is a paragon. . . . Oh, it is all very well for a barber to become skillful enough to shave off a man's beard without his noticing it; but when it comes to a matter which is expressly intended to wound, the acquisition of such skill in applying it so that it will not be noticed—that is revolting."* Quite so. And one of the very hopeful things about the Church today is the growing number of seeking laymen who want to wrestle with some of these difficult propositions of the gospel. In all probability ministers will discover a more enthusiastic reception of theological study and discussion than they realize, and some of the very brilliant young preachers I know are having a most stimulating time through their classes with their laymen.

In all of this we must stay close to the Bible. Daniel Jenkins has a good word for us: "But what above else we have to be is men who are able to move familiarly about the world of the Bible, because we have clear and tested principles with which to interpret it, and are living embodiments of the tradition of the great church through the ages set down in the midst of a particular congregation." In this message to Congregational ministers concerning the communication of the

* *Journal.*

gospel, Jenkins has certainly put down one true word for all of us.

Yet, the center of it all has to be the person of Christ, and we dare not get far away from him. Alfred North Whitehead is quoted by Norman Pittinger* as saying: "The essence of Christianity is the appeal to the life of Christ as a revelation of the nature of God and of his agency in the world. The record is fragmentary, inconsistent and uncertain . . . but there can be no doubt as to what elements in the record have evoked a response from all that is best in human nature. The Mother, the Child, and the bare manger: the lowly man, homeless and self-forgetful, with his message of peace, love, and sympathy; the suffering, the agony, the tender words as life ebbed, the final despair: and the whole with the authority of supreme victory." Yes, there it is.

Yet, it is our task to put in simple words and direct speech some of these great doctrines which undergird us. Remember that Kierkegaard said one time that when he asked Hegel for a street address in Copenhagen, the philosopher gave him a map of Europe. We are the fellows who provide the street addresses, and we are the men who should have experience so that we may say as John Wesley said so often in his *Journal:* "All experience as well as Scripture shows." The Bible itself is the great book of experience and personal testimony, and it is on this we stand.

I take some pride in remembering that the Methodist hymns are nearly all theological. The early Methodists were not learned men for the most part, and Charles Wesley wrote the underlying doctrines of the Methodist Revival into the hymns the people sang and we still sing. Perhaps this is the best place to put our theology, for it seems to me there is

* *Religion in Life,* Autumn 1965, 500-510.

more point to singing what we believe than in simply recit-
ing a creed. Certainly English Methodist scholars have no
hesitancy in quoting a Charles Wesley hymn to illustrate a
doctrine and even to support a position.

Charles Schulz, who draws "Peanuts," brings a good deal of
religion into his column and newspaper readers seem to like
it. Some time ago, Linus and Lucy were looking out the
window into a hard rain. Lucy said, "Boy, look at it rain . . .
What if it floods the whole world?" Linus replied, "It will
never do that . . . in the ninth chapter of Genesis, God promised Noah that would never happen again and the sign of the
promise is the rainbow . . ." She said, "You've taken a great
load off my mind . . ." and Linus replied, "Sound theology
has a way of doing that." Perhaps this is a good place to stop
in our discussion of the minister as a theologian. The minds
of modern men will be healed by sound theology, and it is
the responsibility and the privilege of the minister to apply
that healing. This obligation will not bring us much comfort,
but it may increase our sense of the importance of our
calling.

VI THE EVANGELIST

Then Philip opened his mouth, and
beginning with this scripture he told
him the good news of Jesus.

Acts 8:35

To my Methodist forebearers it would have
sounded ridiculous to set aside for special consideration the
office of evangelist in the Christian ministry. To them
preaching was evangelism, and the preacher was always seeking conversions to the Christian faith. At best, this subject
should have been a subtopic under preaching in general, and
to have assumed that it was worthy of being regarded as a
separate world of the minister would not have been understood. My own point of view is no doubt colored by that
tradition, and it seems to me today that the recovery of this
lost world is one of the essential tasks of the Christian ministry.

If we subscribe to anything like the established church idea
or if we believe in a national church, we are likely to think
that the preacher's task is not primarily evangelistic. A minister of a state church finds his job is keeping records and the
proper observation of national holidays. He will be called

upon to give religious pageantry to the celebration of great and memorable historical occasions. Of course, he is also supposed to keep the moral law and the duties of ethical behavior before the people.

The idea of an establishment does not usually produce vital, living piety. It becomes increasingly difficult to maintain a sense of relevancy in such a religious organization. Thus far in my travels around the world I have yet to see a national church which seemed to me to be the ideal we ought to strive for or to note an established church which did not show signs of emptiness behind its splendid façade. It tends to substitute ritual for life. Sometimes in such a situation, it has been a great relief to go to a Salvation Army meeting where somebody seemed to think that the gospel meant conversion, life, and excitement. It troubles me very much that The Methodist Church in so many places now resembles the Church of England in the eighteenth century when John Wesley and his followers felt a call to try and resurrect the dead.

One thing that seems fairly clear to me is that preaching which is not evangelistic loses its cutting edge. The preacher must think of himself as a man sent to proclaim the good news to every man, and this seems to me to involve conversion and a new direction. We are not proclaiming a code of ethics or a code of morals, but we are offering a new power to live by, a power to overcome and a power to triumph. Sermons which are merely literary accomplishments with proper references to history and appealing to the mind, may provide some small benefit. But preaching must present the claims of Christ to every person, and this involves decision and response. I would insist that preaching is always evangelistic if it is Christian preaching. The Church under the influence of this kind of presentation will become, not a second-rate coun-

try club, but a cavalcade of followers of the Way and a fellowship of believers.

In our time it seems to me particularly necessary that this
oftentimes lost note should be recovered. We cannot leave
this to the sects or to a few professional evangelists. For our
condition is different from that in our fathers' time. Some of
the brethren are talking about the "post-Christian" age, and
while I think this is often grossly exaggerated, they do have a
point. My own belief is that you can never talk about anything "post" until at some point you have achieved it. What
age could ever be called Christian in any honest sense? What
generation ever achieved the right to be called a Christian
generation? What nation can really be called a Christian nation? All of these things are for the future, and the more
carefully one reads his history, the more reluctant he is to
mark periods off as pre or post anything.

A CHURCHLESS WORLD

Still, one thing quite clear to me is an increasing number
of people among us who have had no relationship with a
church and no knowledge of the Bible. We are being confronted by numbers of young people who do not have the
foggiest notion what we are talking about when we make a
reference to a Bible story or refer to a biblical idea. They
have heard nothing about the Book in their homes, and they
never have darkened the door of a Sunday School. One meets
older people who have been outside Christian institutional
life from the beginning and only know about it from what
they read in the papers or hear on the radio. You can imagine
what kind of a distorted point of view they have about the
whole enterprise.

There was a time when much of our evangelism was really

an appeal to nostalgia. Nearly everyone who heard us had a praying mother or a righteous father. They may have drifted far from their childhood training, but there was a chord you could touch and vibrate with memory. Oftentimes it brought them back into the Church for which they realized suddenly they were homesick. That becomes less and less common and our approach must be different. We are face to face with the hard fact that there are many people with whom we shall have to begin at the beginning and who have no childhood experiences for us to build on or recall.

This is not altogether a disadvantage. There have been so many people in our society inoculated with a rather mild Christianity and this vaccination made them impervious to the real thing. There were others who had such false impressions gleaned from a fundamentalist background that much time had to be spent in eliminating outgrown and childish concepts before they could build a living faith. Anyone who travels very much and does not confess that he is a minister in every conversation, or does not wear a clerical collar, will listen to more nonsense talked about religion than on most any other subject in the world. On the basis of a few childish concepts a man or a woman will hold forth as if they were Ph.D.'s in the field. This is very embarrassing to a man on a plane who does not have the time or the energy to give a whole course in the Christian faith before the end of the journey. Sometimes it has seemed to me it would be a much better thing to talk to somebody who comes without any preconceptions and to share with him what the Christian faith has meant to me. If the biblical reference does not ring a familiar bell in the ears of a good many people today, neither does pious boredom set in when they hear one of those dramatic and wonderful encounters recorded in the

Old Testament or New Testament.

Our task becomes more and more the task of the early Christian missionary in the Roman Empire. We proclaim a way that has to be explained. We offer a gift that has to be defined. We shout out some good news that has to be justified. It becomes less practical to maintain ourselves by just warming up cold Christians or transferring church members from one church where they have had a bad experience to our church where they haven't had one yet but probably will in the future. This seems to me to say that evangelism has to be the center of the whole process once again if the Church is to grow and society is not to be captured by some pagan way. And this is true not only for the fellow over in the vacant lot in a tent who is holding a two-week meeting, but for the cultured gentleman who fills the pulpit of the rich and traditional church on the avenue.

A few years ago when I was in Russia as leader of a group of travelers, we were assigned a guide who would stay with us in a certain city for a few days and then we would be met by another young person at our next stop. Some of these youngsters were very attractive physically and mentally, and I welcomed every opportunity to sit next to them on the bus trips and talk. They were atheists without exception and sure that the decadent ways of the West were proved hopeless by superstitious religion. Yet, they were guiding us and they were polite, so that the combination made it very easy to talk about Christianity from my own experience. They had so many wrong impressions (from my viewpoint) that I had to tell them about the history of the Church and its accomplishments. I talked about who Christ was and what I believed about him. So far as I know there were no conversions made, but in my prayers I remember those young people and hope that some word spoken may have lodged in minds which one day would remember a testimony and a faith. But I thought at the time how difficult it would be to have to do Christian work in Russia, providing it were allowed. You would have to start at the beginning as the early Christians did and build the foundation.

That situation does not exist in America as yet, but it becomes more apparent all the time. Preaching will have to deal with the fundamentals of the gospel much more than it has in the past. We must assume less and less about the knowledge of the congregation, and we must become more adequate in defining the simple steps of Christian commitment. Perhaps our textbook will become the Book of Acts again and our examples will be men like St. Paul who, it is reported, "argued in the synagogue with the Jews and the devout persons, and in the market place every day with those who chanced to be there" (Acts 17:17).

This will demand some hard, and many times, new thinking about how to break through into the world. I suppose this is what is being talked about when Christian writers use such terms as "worldly holiness" and "secular Christianity." The only objection to these ideas is the arrogance of their promoters. They want us to believe the ideas were discovered today and they are the prophets of radically new concepts. They have been developing quite a long time, and there have been other ages when the Church faced very similar problems. But it is clear enough that we must develop techniques, and more important than that, the will and the desire to be Christian missionaries again or, as I would prefer to say, become Christian evangelists.

RECOLLECTIONS

When I was a boy my parents took me to a good many revival meetings. In the California towns where I grew up, one of the winter events was usually a "protracted meeting" which lasted anywhere from two to six weeks. An outstanding evangelist would come to town with a music director and set up a large tent with sawdust on the floor and hard benches for the congregation to sit on. For at least two or three nights a week our family would be there, and while my brother and I would fall asleep before it was all over, we helped fill the seats. These were very pleasant experiences for the most part because of the singing. Usually there was a large choir, and nearly always they had somebody who knew how to get the people to sing. The songs were the old revival types which I am told are usually very poor music. That may be, but they had a swing and a lilt which was a very adequate substitute for jazz for me and the older folks. One thing I noted about those songs was that they were all positive and full of hope. They had found an answer and it was proclaimed with assurance and enthusiasm.

Yet, these revival meetings were not so much evangelistic as they were a method of Christian nurture. To this day, especially in the South, there are meetings held for a week or so in many churches, and this is a regular part of the program. There are a few honest-to-God sinners who are converted, and there are people who make a first commitment to the Christian way. But the main purpose of the meeting is to warm up Christians who have grown cold and to remind them who they are and what Christian faith ought to be in their lives. It was assumed in the days of my boyhood, and it is still assumed in some places, that no church can keep alive and alert to its opportunities and responsibilities without this extra "shot in the arm" at least once a year. This reawakening and reheating of church members is one of the main contributions coming out of Billy Graham's meetings. Revivalism, in other words, was not only evangelism but it was pastoral care and the nurture of Christians already committed to the faith.

My boyhood experiences of revivals, however, represented the end of something. In college everybody assumed that this kind of religion was dead, never to be revived. The students and professors lived in a different world, and even those of us who came from homes with this evangelistic background never talked about it and assumed that college was an experience which would make that kind of religion irrelevant. It is true that when Dr. Graham appeared upon the scene, he revived a hope that this old method of winning people was still a live option, but there are not very many Grahams and other organizations such as his. Billy Graham seems to me an example of what a man with particular gifts, particular convictions, and particular dedication can accomplish in any time if dedicated to Jesus Christ. I doubt that it means we are at the beginning of a new cycle of the kind of meetings I remember from my boyhood.

So far as I can recall, at the theological seminary I attended there was never a word spoken about evangelism. I do not say this with any criticism because my seminary filled me with many riches which I could never repay and for which I am forever thankful. But evangelism was not one of the subjects that was taught directly or indirectly. We were to be scholars and learn a little about administering a church school and do the best we could with our preaching. This was a day when emotion was frowned upon in any field and especially in the preacher's approach to the sinner. Revivalism had left a bad odor, and there was a general assumption that its passing was not a cause for regret.

Our faith was given to education, and in those days the bright young men were going to be religious educators. Using the same methods that the secular teachers used, we intended to win the new generation to Christianity and the Church by understanding the correct educational procedures. One heard about "preaching missions" in some churches, which were really a watered-down revival meeting. Somebody from outside came in to preach for three or four days, but nothing like a call to commitment or to repentance was ever made. It was hoped that a fresh voice might do something to awaken the sluggishness of church members.

In the annual conference of The Methodist Church, no one wanted to be on the Board of Evangelism because it would associate him with ministers who were not modern. It was an honor to be elected to the Board of Education or to the Board of Social Action, but evangelism was not where the action was. It seems rather strange, as we look back upon it, that at the very time when advertising was using every kind of emotional appeal and political movements were winning converts with slogans, the Church turned away from the emotional. The Church suddenly became an institution suspicious of any mention of blood, sweat, and tears and dedicated itself to the proposition that by educational methods alone people would be encouraged to make their commitments to Christ.

In my own ministry there was a growing concern that something had been left out and that something very significant had to be rediscovered. Some years later in a Midwestern pulpit it was necessary for me to be the host for a school of evangelism dedicated to the visitation method. These were the days when we rediscovered something in the New Testament which had long been neglected. Laymen were trained to go out two by two to call on families and hopefully lay before them the claims of the Christian faith. I was not enthusiastic about this, but being the host, there was no choice but to cooperate. It was a great experience to discover that my laymen could come back and report that here was a family that was outside the Church and now ready to come into it. I was to call upon them and make the arrangements. Suddenly with the impact of a new conversion, it came to me that my ministry was to win people to Christ and there was no real joy for the preacher who was not fulfilling this part of his task. It was out of that experience that evangelism became my concern, and now whenever I am referred to as an evangelist, it fills me with delight.

OUR PRESENT SITUATION

If one thing seems clear to me it is that there is a constant change of mood within the churches. Every few years there is suddenly something indefinable yet very real in the air. In my own lifetime there seems to have been three distinctive moods in the Church. In the beginning of my ministry, it was a scientific spirit, which cast a jaundiced eye toward theology and at the Church as an institution. No one claimed that the tide was running our way and no one felt that we were in any ways riding a crest of popularity or enjoying a general acceptance. The war changed this mood.

Who can ever describe the situation of churches during the war and immediately afterward! In many places in Europe and especially in England, the Church suffered badly and there was a great decline in support and membership. Not so in America. During the war itself there was a rediscovery of the significance of religion and a general willingness to hear the preacher proclaim an eternal, comforting world if not always a willingness to listen to a prophetic word. War brought with it a sense of the tragedy of human life. It gave men a feeling there were things they could not control and issues beyond their solution. This is more or less the case in times of great national disaster and crisis.

After the war people turned back to the churches in large numbers, and no one seemed to know why. New churches were built. Young couples brought their children back into the church school, but they stayed themselves and these young families became the central strength of new congregations which sprang up in so many places in the nation. People were going to church in larger numbers, and wherever there was anything happening at all, there were full sanctuaries on Sunday. Money was easy and budgets were subscribed and oversubscribed. We never had it so good in many ways, and on the American scene, at least, Christianity had a hearing from the President on down.

Now we have entered a different time and we are facing a different situation. The good times are over and the ministry has to fight for its life in many places. This new mood seems to have affected the theologian and the preacher more than it has the layman. There arises a general cry of dissatisfaction with the old and radical new demands for change. The Church as an institution is discounted and dismissed from within while theologians pontificate on what has to be said now with no apparent understanding of what has happened in the past under similar circumstances.

This, at the present time, is what might be called a failure of nerve. It is the kind of spirit which overtook the Roman Empire during the period that Christianity arrived upon the scene. If one wants to be drowned in pessimism, he does not need to listen to the attack of the world or heed atheism's boastful assertions. Let him listen to the hired servants of the Church themselves and he will soon wonder how any institution can expect leadership from such voices.

There seems to be a loss of confidence in the message. There is a haunting suspicion that Christianity has nothing to say to an urban situation or to a Christian fellowship exiled to the inner city. There is a general lack of confidence in the ministry and its function. It is almost as if the medical profession should suddenly confess that it is nothing but an association of quacks who will do the best they can but it has nothing in the way of real healing to offer. It is as if an organization of lawyers confessed they are nothing but shysters with no ability to help people understand the law or attain justice. There seems to be a general disease which has infected us and causes us to discount ourselves, our profession, and our proclamation.

It has always been one of the Church's chief strengths that its critics are from within it. Good healthy criticism is not the sign of weakness but of strength. This today, however, is something different and it reflects not an attack on the second-rate in the light of the best, but a bitter condemnation of the Church as something without relevancy or hope for the future. The kind of stuff that is pouring forth from preachers' magazines and from training centers for the ministry is enough to make us wonder what has happened to the ministry. What happened to the call of God to serve within the ranks of a fellowship against which our Lord said the gates of hell could not prevail?

Simone Weil, French writer and mystic, said one time, "I should be more willing to die for the church, if it should ever need one to die for it, than to join it." This is a rather widely held sentiment, apparently, and is characteristic always of those whose mystical religion can never come to terms with the hard and difficult facts of organized religious life. This is one of the main reasons why John Wesley was so critical of the mystics in general. He thought they had no proper appreciation of the Church, and he knew as every churchman knows that a rather soft, tender, and amorphous sentiment will have a hard time dealing with the often frustrating activities of a group of Christians who have not been made perfect. The minister, however, has to be tough enough to live in these two worlds at the same time. Not for him that vague, amorphous, undisciplined fellowship offered to us by the "underground church."

We need to come to a fresh realization that the Church as an institution is the base from which is launched any attack we are to make on the world in the name of Jesus Christ. Whether we like it or not, we cannot long endure without some place of support and defense when our invasion into the various pagan provinces is turned back. The professional evangelist may be critical of the Church, but without it he will not last long. The minister who understands evangelism as a main part of his task will soon find out that when men hear his word and respond to it, there must be some fellowship he can introduce them to for their continual growth.

We have made a good deal of progress in many of our Protestant churches in training our members and educating people into the meaning of the Church and the Christian faith. In many a church nobody can join by just accepting an invitation that is given by the minister. They must sign up for a course of several weeks and spend at least one night each week studying what Christian discipleship means and what church membership implies. One of the great evangelists of our time, Dr. Harry Denman, said one time that when Saul had his experience on the Damascus Road and became Paul the Christian, the other disciples were very slow in believing him sincere and in accepting him. Denman said they were opposed to anyone who had not gone through the membership class. Yet a church is certainly on the right track when it spends more time in training its new members and making sure that those who join do not become only names on a roll.

John Wesley, however, seems to have reversed this order, and while he made it very easy for people to get into the fellowship, he made it very hard for them to stay in. Holiness was not an entrance requirement, and Wesley made the perfectly valid assumption that men come into a church not because they are saints but because they are sinners. So all seeking membership had to indicate was a desire to "flee from the wrath to come," and this openness created a world church.

But the early Methodists were very severe in their demands, and it was not at all unusual for people to be expelled from their fellowship. This was done after first confronting the individual with the charges against him and a demand for repentance. The Church was thought of as an institution with a wide-open door for the newcomer and the sinner, but as a place of high demand for the one who remained.

The insistence upon striving after holiness of life and a passionate seeking after a personal experience of God is the mark of a Christian fellowship which has the authentic evangelistic point of view. This is not characteristic of religions regarded as merely a social force. In the nineteenth century Lord Melbourne, who was a decent enough man and a good prime minister, was always nervous at the idea of any enthusiasm, especially in the established church. He did not like it either in religion or any other place, and his great dislike of the Dissenters was chiefly because of their enthusiasm. He said, "If we are to have a prevailing religion, let us have one that is cool, and indifferent, and such a one as we have got. . . ."* We are in danger of this prevailing point of view, and if Christianity is to be a lively faith, we shall have to find a different road from the one we now follow.

TECHNIQUES

There seems to be a general assumption in our time that our weakness in the field of evangelism is due to wrong methods. There may be some truth in this, but to believe we are going to cure our weakness by finding a different method is sentimental and unreal. A method is never more than a means to an end, and it can never be the recovery of a sense of direction or of a sense of reality.

There is much talk in the churches about the "old methods" not working any more. An old method seems to be anything that has been tried previously, and some young ministers shout out that this is no longer valid. I sometimes wonder how they know, since they have never tried either the old methods or any other method. Knowing nothing about the answer to our contemporary problem, we take a strange kind of comfort out of proclaiming that at least we know nothing that worked previously will work now.

While mass evangelism demands a special kind of person

* Melbourne Papers, March 1800.

and a special kind of organization, we cannot play down the amazing spectacle of thousands of people coming together in the name of religion. In 1963 when Billy Graham was in Los Angeles, I was the chairman of the local committee. Dr. Graham's more conservative brethren attacked him vigorously for allowing a heretic like me to be associated with him. My more progressive brethren voiced a disapproval of my showing any interest in his movement and objected to my support of it. I am a strong believer in the ability of Christians to work together for common purposes when they do not always agree on theology. I still take considerable pleasure in remembering that the closing meeting of that campaign was held in the Los Angeles Coliseum and there were 150,000 people present. It was the largest gathering of people in the history of the well-known arena, and it gives me some satisfaction to know that it was not an athletic event or a political rally but a Protestant religious meeting. In some places and under some circumstances apparently this old method still works.

Here and there, there are happenings which must excite any Christian. Surely, the Kirkentag in Germany is an event worth noticing. Alan Walker's "life line" in Sydney, Australia, and his "Christian cabaret" for young people on Saturday night in the same city, are exciting things. A young man from the National Council of Churches in Las Vegas spends his time in the night spots, being available to troubled people—something worth noting. Evangelism through drama is being practiced in my part of the country, and there are other places where it is being done as well. The Methodist Board of Evangelism sends a team to Daytona Beach, Florida, and Palm Springs, California, during Easter Week and uses all kinds of unconventional approaches. When a large bureaucracy of a large institution dares to experiment with rad- ical new ways, it must mean that Christians are not altogether hopeless so far as being open to new methods is concerned.

We act sometimes as if ours was the first generation to think of reaching people through new methods. Actually, it goes back as far as some of the dramatic actions of the great proph- ets. In my communion we tend to forget that the beginnings of street preaching and field preaching took place because the churches were closed to the early Methodist preachers. John Wesley, the Oxford don, did not make the adjustment easily and in his *Journal* for April 2, 1739, he writes: "At four in the afternoon, I submitted to be more vile, and proclaimed in the highways the glad tidings of salvation, speaking from a little eminence in a ground adjoining to the city, to about three thousand people." There on Haddam Mount outside Bristol, our English brethren have placed a pulpit to mark the first field preaching of Wesley, who did it not gladly but out of compulsion. Every age will demand its own approach, and the Christian Church must forever be aware of the method and technique which will unlock the door to the hearts of the people. There is no need to talk about some- thing brand new in evangelism because it is always necessary to find the fresh way in every generation. New occasions do teach new duties, but more important than the technique is the living evangelistic spirit at the center of the Christian experience.

There are a few general principles which we should have in mind to guide us as we study our techniques. One which seems to me quite obvious is that there is no sense in talking about the good old days which were not so good as we re- member and in any case cannot be recalled. We have to come to terms with the contemporary situation and with the mood of the people. A Jewish commentator says that when the Old Testament refers to the God of Abraham, Isaac, and Jacob, it is saying that He is a God who is always the same and yet ever relevant to each generation. The Christian gospel must not forget that biblical proposition.

The minister must use plain language, and he must do more listening than it is easy for men in our profession to do. The Church has often failed in its responsibility for Christian nurture. It is the members of many a Christian fellowship who have become the field of evangelism rather than being the troops with which we can overcome the world. The minister ought to have a core of people within the organization who have learned what being a Christian means and are able to present it to other laymen with effectiveness and directness. The picture of a Christian church as merely a group of listeners is a denial of its nature. Some of us have found from experience that laymen are the very best evangelists in many situations and that the minister's task as evangelist is to be a teacher of small groups of lay evangelists.

The Church must not be afraid to try some experiments which may not show any statistical result. This can be carried too far, but there must be places where we move into society with no hope of advancing the Church as an institution. On this path there will be many failures and we should expect them. The Christian minister who is doing his job always has some far-out experiments going on in the hopes that he may stumble on something to break through the defenses of a secular society.

Evangelism in our times becomes more and more social in its implications. Even those who are traditionally committed to the individual approach are learning that life in the last half of the twentieth century does not allow anyone to live that kind of life nor does it encourage anyone to preach that kind of gospel. The social witness is always evangelistic ultimately, for it is a proclamation of the relevance of the Christian faith to men caught in the political and social entanglements of the day.

In the nineteenth century Lord Shaftesbury was one of the great philanthropists. Probably disliked as much as any politician of the Victorian Age, he kept putting his nose into such things as the sewers of London, the hovels of Dorset, the mills of Manchester, and the mines of Durham. He made inquiries about children in factories or up chimneys, about lunatics in asylums, about the condition of needlewomen, about burglars and pickpockets. He encouraged the ragged schools for the poor children, and he read Bible lessons at services held in theaters. He was representative of the brethren who believe the gospel must be in the world and speak directly to the victims of the world. He can teach us a great deal in our time, and he will be witness that not all love of the secular world began with us. Amos can teach us the same thing, for that matter.

Evangelism, no matter how iconoclastic, ought to be in good taste. The shocking vulgarity which some well-meaning proclaimers of the gospel are using, will not in the long run accomplish good things. The Church has some responsibility for taste, and even when the tide seems to be flowing in the other direction, we will not be serving God or man properly if we encourage the profane and shocking. When, for example, in a certain city a theater under the auspices of the churches has a naked male dancer appear before the audience in order to symbolize a man standing naked before God, we are impressed only with how utterly ridiculous some Christian leaders can be. The newspaperman who wrote about it was impressed only with the fact that you could not see this kind of thing happening in joints usually associated with homosexual entertainment.

Years ago I observed that in public gatherings such as service clubs, the off-color story is resented and the risqué reference strikes no response. Let the Church firmly shut the door against all of this business and while showing no prudery in its relationship with the evil of the world, neither show any cheap attempt to win approbation by getting down into the gutter. Wallowing in the mud will not get us a serious hearing. We have already observed a Christian minister and a Congressman censured and expelled from that body for behavior not proper for a member of Congress, to say nothing of his status as a minister of a Christian church. Let us have no more of it.

THE ART OF EVANGELISM

The man who will be an evangelist in his preaching and in his witnessing is not necessarily an authority on all the things men are interested in. Keats, it has been pointed out, has Cortez staring out across the Pacific with a wild surmise, sighted upon a peak in Darien. He had the wrong man, for it was Balboa, but this does not subtract anything significant from the wonder of his poem and the truth of his insight. So the Christian evangelist is the man who has the authentic experience, and this is the essential thing.

Clifford Odets said, "A playwright who writes about things that he is not connected with, or to, is not a creative writer. He may be a very skilled writer, and it may be on a very high level of craft, but he is not going to be what I call an artist, a poet." This is the heart of it, and the preacher who is "connected with" what he is talking about is a man who has the authority as well as the artistry. This entering into the experience in a real way and bearing witness to its authentic nature is the heart of what I call evangelistic effectiveness. This creates enthusiasm, and there is nothing so contagious as the enthusiastic spirit. Horace Bushnell defined this kind of witness when he wrote: "No great work of genius was ever written in the way of work, or before the wings were lifted by some gale of inspiration; which gale, again, would never have begun to blow, had not the windows of thought the chambers of light and beauty within been open, by years of patient toil and study. The artist plods on wearily, drudging in the details of his art, till finally the inspiration takes him, and from that point onward his hand is moved by his subject, with no conscious drudgery or labor."* Bushnell has another word that is helpful here. He is talking about the moderates whom he refers to as "the wooden-headed school, who dread nothing with so great reason as a combustion of any sort. Hence it is a real problem with them to divide distances and settle themselves down as nearly midway between the poles as possible. Sometimes they are called in derision, men of the fence, but they call themselves, and more correctly, *neuters,* that is, neithers; for the real study and problem of their school is negative. It is not to find the truth as a positive form and law, but it is simply to find a position half way. . . ."†

The evangelist is the man who believes that the gospel has an answer to man's deepest questions. He is like a man who has been freed from some evil habit, and he cannot keep from telling every other man in its grip the good news of how to be free. Personal witnessing is the power and strength of evangelistic preaching.

We see it in John Wesley's experience as he finally came to

* *Horace Bushnell,* edited by H. S. Smith, Oxford, 1965, p. 231.
† *Ibid.,* p. 113.

that moment when he could believe that what Christ had done was "for me." The Evangelical Revival was to a large extent this appropriation by many people of the good news personally and individually. I never cease to marvel at the power a preacher has when he can say that it happened to him and that his proclamation is not an abstraction but a concrete report being delivered to a particular man.

This is to recover a sense of the urgency of our task, and nothing much can happen until we find this personal authority. The weakness of so much of our preaching is simply that it is a kind of emotionless discussion of a general proposition that is only mildly interesting. The preacher with power is an evangelist at heart who preaches in Baxter's unforgettable words: "as never sure to preach again, and as a dying man to dying men."

John Wesley was under attack constantly from the bishops because of his irregular procedures. His defense was always a matter of pointing to the results obtained and the failure of the more orthodox methods to achieve these results. On the 11th of June in 1747, he wrote a letter to the Bishop of London, replying to criticisms made against him: "The habitual drunkard that was, is now temperate in all things; the whoremonger now flees fornication; he that stole, steals no more, but works with his hands; he that cursed or swore, perhaps at every sentence, has now learned to serve the Lord with fear, and rejoice in him with reverence; those formerly enslaved to vicious habits of sin are now brought to uniform habits of holiness. These are demonstrable facts; I can name the men, with their places of abode." Evangelism ultimately is an assumption that lives ought to be changed by the Christian faith. Evangelistic preaching has the underlying assumption that men do not need to leave the church as they came, but may be visited by some great surprise. Because so much of our preaching is not like this, we are always seeking some way to get the job done in a different way.

In *The Humiliation of the Church,* Van den Heuvel, a secretary of the World Council of Churches, writes in all seriousness that the congregation should be split up into mixed groups of about fifteen people and these groups are to rotate the preaching ministry. The group comes together with the minister, listens to an exegesis of a passage of Scripture, meditates, and then comes to a group decision on the important questions it raises. A layman may be responsible for the final draft, and the final product does not need to be delivered by the minister. The minister's chief contribution is to be theological. He may do the exegetical and doctrinal work on the sermon, but he need not deliver it, and this, mind you, is presented as an advance on preaching. If one can be fairly certain of anything, it is that God hardly ever speaks through a committee. The Word of God comes to us through a spokesman He has put His hand upon and commanded. Does this man know that Layman's Sunday is oftentimes a day when attendance is very low?

I look back often to my teaching predecessor at the Pacific School of Religion, Dr. Carl S. Patton. In a book written in 1938* he said: ". . . though there are many things that can and should be done in a church, other people than the minister can do most of them. One thing he and nobody else can do, and that is the preaching. If he cannot do this he will soon have no Boy Scouts to supervise, no bills to audit, no reports to file, no anything at all. Everything depends on him as a preacher." Amen!

Preaching, of course, is a part of the Church, and the

* *The Preparation and Delivery of Sermons,* Willett, Clark.

preacher is the man who has been anointed by God and appointed by the congregation to this task. Paul said, "For since, in the wisdom of God, the world did not know God through wisdom, it pleased God through the folly of what we preach to save those who believe" (1 Cor. 1:21). No, this is our task alone, and it is for us to find the right word and the right emphasis. Until we become evangelists in our hearts, I fear we shall lack power in our pulpits.

Writing about his memories of Toscanini, Milton Katims said: "Another great facet of the Maestro's genius was his making us feel that no matter how many times we might have played a work, this was the *first* time we were playing it, the *first* time we were really hearing it. He was constantly restudying his scores, so no matter how many times he had conducted a work, *this* was the definitive performance. When we had finished recording the Beethoven Ninth in 1952, and as we sat on stage listening to the final playback, Maestro quietly said to me: 'I have conducted this symphony for fifty years. Fifty years! And, finally, I think I understand something!' Yes, this is why his performances always had such freshness and spontaneity."*

So the preacher who speaks not only from his mind but from his heart is always fresh and exciting. For always he is the messenger and the witness of God's good news of redemption. For him the preaching of the Word is a privilege which is "sweeter as the years go by." He is the evangelist.

* *Saturday Review*, Mar. 25, 1967.

VII THE TEACHER

> For this I was appointed . . . a teacher of
> the Gentiles in faith and truth.
> —1 Timothy 2:7

The minister is involved in teaching always
either directly or indirectly. When a young man starts out in
a small church, he finds himself actively engaged in the church
school program and probably deeply involved with the youth
program on Sunday evening. He may look forward to the
time when with a larger staff he will not be entirely responsible for this particular part of the church's task. I am convinced, however, that if he thinks he can divorce himself
from it completely, he is mistaken. Part of the task of the
minister is to be a teacher of his people, and when he abdi-
cates this responsibility, the result is always sad.

We are involved today in a reexamination of our Christian
Education program, and there is much weeping and wailing
among the experts. The truth is that we are not doing so well
in most places and numbers are falling off. No one seems to
have a clear idea as to what the difficulty is, but we are no
longer riding a constantly rising crest of attendance and par-
ticipation in our local churches.

In my own lifetime I have seen religious education go up and down, and in my seminary days it reached a crest. Those were the days when much glamor covered the religious educator, and hardly anybody wanted to do the ordinary parish work of the minister. In that time we were going to save the world through education. Interestingly enough, it was an education modeled after the secular philosophy of John Dewey. He was our patron saint, and in my seminary we spent more time studying secular philosophies of education than we did the Bible. At the best, the Bible was to be a resource book, which meant that when everything else had failed we might look into it. We damned it with faint praise.

Through the years we have tried to find the latest word that would help us teach the Christian faith to the new generation, that is, providing we believed it could be taught. Like most educational courses, religious education was boring and hopelessly bogged down in generalities and abstractions. Jacques Barzun exploded the whole business when in 1945 he wrote *Teacher in America* and developed the theme that educational theory was a thing of the ivory tower but teaching was at the center of the action.

The truth seems to be that the promises of education in the thirties never materialized so far as the churches were concerned. We did improve certain standards, and we put more emphasis on teacher training. But there has arisen an increasing cry for more Bible in our curriculum, and a large number of church teachers took an increasingly dim view toward teaching Christianity as just one subject among many. In 1941 Shelton Smith published his book, *Faith and Nurture,* and I heard him give some of the lectures which were expanded in this book. His point was that the religion being taught in democracy was an anthropocentric experimentalism which in its fundamental assumptions was far from the Christian faith. He called for Christian educators more aware of their responsibility to nurture old and young in the Hebrew-Christian religion. The main effect of the book, so far as I was concerned, was a reaffirmation of the necessity of a theological undergirding of Christian education. We could not expect the public school system to endorse such an approach, but the Church was responsible for proclaiming and continuing it now as always.

There have been very few fields in which there has been so much ferment recently as in the field of education. This is all to the good, and if today the Church once again has to reexamine its responsibilities and its methods, we should all rejoice. The minister must be aware of this ferment, and while he probably will not play the part of an expert, he must certainly be in it as one who is committed to the proclamation, presentation, and demonstration of ideas often caught from charismatic individuals. But Christian education must also be taught by more pedestrian exponents of the faith.

This changing of the spirit and approach to education is oftentimes in the spirit of the London *Times*. After many years of its famous front-page personal columns and lists of births, marriages, and death announcements, suddenly it tries to become like its rivals. As Mollie Panter-Downes remarked in *The New Yorker*,* "Though the new get up has its admirers, many sorrowful readers feel that it becomes *The Times* as uneasily as a mini-skirt would sit on a mature blue stocking —as unflatteringly, truth to tell, as most of London's current crop of clothes strike one as one walks along the streets this Summer of the Thigh, brooding over the basic British figure structures they so startlingly reveal." The Church's desperate

* July 9, 1966.

attempt to "get with it" oftentimes turns out to be as passing and ephemeral as the change of a fashion. A part of St. Augustine's task as the Bishop of Hippo in the fifth century was to teach young Christians some basic things about the Christian faith. This is still the basic task of the Church, and the Church's ministry should not regard a new style as anything more than it actually is. Usually it is merely a change of method.

It may be that we as Christians are back nearer to the task of the early days of the Church than we are to the past generation. There is more demand for basic Christian teaching and for basic Christian proclamation because of the number of people who have had no indoctrination at all. In some ways the Christian minister becomes more like the Christian missionary every day, and the missionary's task includes a larger element of teaching than the pastor of an American church is likely to have experienced.

As long as statistics were on our side, in spite of some very troublesome developments all around us, we could take the attitude of a psychiatrist who was asked one time whether he had ever been psychoanalyzed. He replied, "No, I want to let well enough alone." I do not regard the present crisis, therefore, as a total loss. On the contrary, it will force us to examine our own faith and our own methods of proclaiming it, so that the Church will be forced to emphasize smaller groups talking with the teacher more than it has in the days past.

Our environment is one of high respect, indeed almost worship, of the educational process. This is no new thing. Agnes Repplier said in 1931: "The United States is a country of diverse theologies and of one creed, of many churches and of one temple, of a thousand theories and of one conviction. The creed is education, the temple is the schoolhouse, and the conviction is the healing power of knowledge. Rich and poor, pretentious and plain, revivalist and atheist, all share this supreme and touching confidence. Our belief in education is unbounded, our reverence for it is unfaltering, our loyalty to it is unshaken by reverses. Our passionate desire, not so much to acquire it as to bestow it, is the most animated of American traits. The ideal democracy is an educated democracy; and our naïve faith in the moral intelligibility of an established order makes clear the path of progress. Of all the money expended by the government, the billions it pays for the instruction of youth seems to us to be a most profitable outlay."* If the Church does not share completely this point of view, and I do not believe it should, it must at least understand that teaching is an essential part of its witness if it is to possess the future.

That the present period in America is not too different from that of thirty-five years ago is indicated by several events on the educational front. For example, Clayton Fritchey, who is primarily a political commentator, pointed out that some of the big universities were offering the big monetary rewards these days.† Arthur Schlesinger, Jr., was offered $100,000 salary to occupy the Albert Schweitzer Chair in Humanities at the City University of New York. He was to be furnished secretaries, researchers, given lots of time to think and travel with all expenses paid. Nothing was mentioned about his responsibility to students and classes. George Kennan at Princeton Institute for Advanced Study became in addition the Harvard University Fellow in History of Slavic Civilizations, which involved apparently an occasional trip to Harvard as a lecturer, but no word about regular class sched-

* *Times and Tendencies,* Houghton, 1931.
† *Harper's,* April 1966.

ules. Richard Goodwin, a special assistant to President Kennedy and President Johnson, and Pat Moynihan, who was a former Assistant Secretary of Labor, are at Wesleyan University with all kinds of free time and no time clocks to punch. Really, teaching seems to be one of the promising activities of the day. The Church can offer no competing possibilities in this field, but it must not disregard the significance of what these happenings say to us. The Church must be a first-rate teaching institution, and it must hold teaching and teachers in high regard.

THE MAIN POINT

In the study of the German attempt and failure in World War II,* the author makes a remark that could well apply to other affairs beside the military. "Marked on a map," says the author, "the conquests of the Wehrmacht were awesome but the combination of decisions that led to them was military madness. He who cannot reject cannot select, and the downfall of the Third Reich was due, in no small measure, to Adolf Hitler's inability to realize that, in strategic terms, the road to everywhere is the road to nowhere." The modern church has oftentimes been guilty of that same error, and its program has been a little of everything which finally ended up by being nothing. We had classes in modern dance and the modern novel, but if a churchman took every one of the courses, he would end up with a smattering of minor skills in scattered matters. There are still enough churches around with great barnlike rooms to remind us of the day when a gymnasium was to win young people, especially the boys, into

* Pelford Taylor, *The Breaking Wave: The Second World War in the Summer of 1940*, Simon & Schuster, 1958.

the kingdom of God. Now the problem is how to use those huge spaces when their original religious purpose has long since been declared futile and ridiculous.

This has been the time of assuming that everything had to be "interesting" or else it could lay no claim to the careful attention of either young people or adults. There has been an assumption that nobody wanted anything that was not amusing, and we missed the point of the difference between the truly dramatic and the merely titillating. Churches have been guilty of playing down to their members, and many a man has decided the evening classes at the community high school were much to be preferred over any of the rather silly activities provided by his own church. St. Paul warned us rightly of the futility of addressing men of the flesh as spiritual and the necessity of feeding babes in Christ with milk rather than with solid food (1 Cor. 3:1-2). It is my conviction, however, that we have assumed that nobody ever grew up in the Christian churches and that our parishioners not only were unable to digest meat but were actually more anxious to be served milk. It comes as a shock to some religious leaders to realize that it is just as serious a mistake to underestimate capacity as it is to overestimate it.

One of the things that impresses a reader of old sermons is the kind of people they demanded as their hearers. There is nothing light about them nor is there any conscious attempt to make them interesting and understandable. They are heavy-going and full of theological explanations which are not always easy even for the man who has been through seminary. Yet, some of the men who preached those sermons talked to the common people and were heard gladly.

Let us assume at once that this heavy preaching will not be gladly heard in our time. But let us assume also that the essential nature of man has not changed to the extent we have assumed. As I look back over my experiences, I am astounded at the number of laymen who responded eagerly to anything like a serious discussion of some of the theological fundamentals of the Christian faith. If I were to begin again, I would make a more conscious provision in my ministry for the people who want to become mature followers of the Master. I would pay more attention to the intellectually curious among the flock.

Many years ago there was a family who attended my services regularly. Their name was Davis and they lived on a farm about fifteen miles out of town, and yet even in the worst winter weather they would be in their place. The father told me one time that he had no formal education to speak of, and as I recall, he had never gone beyond the sixth grade. But he was anything but a stupid man, as I found out to my delight. Once in a while when he came to town to buy supplies during the week, he would call at my office somewhat hesitantly and in the beginning I would see him somewhat reluctantly. But I got over my hesitation because he never stayed very long and there was always some point in last Sunday's sermon that he wanted me to expand a little or clarify. Sometimes he would say to me he had been pondering this point I had made as he rode the tractor up and down the field, and he wondered if maybe a further implication of the idea might be such and such. Always his words revealed a very careful consideration of the subject, and more times than not he uncovered something I had not seen. When I stood in my pulpit on Sunday morning, I would see that family and I would pray within, "O Lord, do not let me say anything today that will sound shallow or foolish to Davis when he is riding his tractor this week." There were university professors in my congregation, too, but somehow I always thought of this man as I tried to expound a conviction or an idea.

I remember another family who were in church with the same regularity. The father was an insurance executive and much better educated than the farmer. When I mentioned to him one time how much it meant to me to have his family present, he said something I have never forgotten: "I regard it as part of my children's education to listen to you preach."

A sermon is not primarily an intellectual discussion but it must always be regarded as a teaching tool. The sermon that does not teach and is regarded merely as inspiration becomes a hollow thing without substance. We must respect the quality of our laymen, and we must never assume that only the man with a Ph.D. is to be preached to intellectually. The educational level of our congregations has risen, no doubt, and we have better educated people to preach to than our fathers knew. But the conflicting claims for their attention is perhaps greater than ever before, and it is for us to speak simply and directly and dramatically, if possible, so that the old story never seems dull.

The Church is one of the few places where some men may hear the other side of the story. There is a kind of monotonous sameness in all the propaganda that pours forth from the newsmen, the movies, the drama, and the hundred and one propaganda mills going full speed. It is in the Church that another side of the question may be presented and a longer look taken. It was said in the New Testament that Jesus crossed over to the other side of the lake, and he was always crossing over to the other side of the great issues facing men. For today we are as confused as ever regarding the meaning of life and find it just as difficult to discover the narrow gate and the strait path that leads to life. The gospel goes contrary to the modern advice filling the air. It is for the Church to present the options facing all men.

The Christian minister ought to have certain classes which he conducts himself and in which he shares the very best he can give his people. If it is not necessary, I think no man ought to teach a Sunday School class just before he preaches, although I did for a long time in my youth. Those minutes belong to the preacher in isolation. But this does not excuse him from having a definite part in the educational program of the church.

I am a strong believer in Bible study, for I believe it is the most exciting Book in the world if it is taught with knowledge and understanding. One of the most popular things I ever did in my churches was to conduct a morning class for the women and an evening study group for anybody who would come. We may be sure that so far as most of the people are concerned, they have had very little chance to go down very deep in this Book and we will be astounded at the eager way many respond.

Perhaps you recall that when someone asked Grumpy of Snow White and the Seven Dwarfs, "How do you do?" he replied, "How do you do what?" And so when we are talking in generalities about teaching in the Church, the proper question is how do you teach what? It cannot be said too often that we teach what we know about the Christian way. The sermon will be doing this, hopefully every Sunday, and the minister will be doing it in different ways and at different times. Pick up a conversation with almost anyone, anywhere, on the subject of religion and you will soon discover that we have not been doing it very much and we have not been doing it very well. It is into this teaching world that the modern minister must enter wholeheartedly and expectantly.

For we have talked so much about the failure of the Christian education program that we have failed to appreciate some of its undoubted virtues. Apparently it is still true that youngsters who attend the church school in spite of its inadequacies oftentimes come out with a certain point of view which is a bulwark against delinquency. A good many years ago when I graduated from college an older friend asked me what I had gotten out of it. He knew that it had taken some effort and sacrifice for me to get through college, and I knew he expected me to give some eloquent and impressive testimony as to its worth. As I thought of it, there came to me a rather simple proposition which I am sure disappointed him. I said college had given me a critical point of view toward what people were saying and believing and an appreciation for truth. This still seems to me to be the heart of it, and what college did for me was to give me a certain attitude. The main purpose of Christian education is to say to our people in the words of St. Paul, "Have this mind among yourselves, which you have in Christ Jesus" (Phil. 2:5).

There is an indefinable, amorphous effect of many important things that we experience. James Q. Wilson, an associate professor of government at Harvard, writes that what we commonly regard as a crime explosion is nothing more or less than a population explosion.* He says more young people every year mean a higher crime rate because young people have a higher crime rate than adults. He forecasts that in Southern California the number of serious crimes will increase in the next ten years by 55 per cent. Then he gives us this optimistic conclusion: "For the present, the only way we know of fighting crime is birth control."

* *The Public Interest,* Fall Issue, 1966.

Our fathers might have thought that the best way to handle this problem is through a second birth. They would have said that everybody needs to be born again and that once is not enough. If we are not doing our job as well as it ought to be done, and certainly we are not, then let us face it and analyze it to the best of our ability. But let us not surrender to what seems inevitable simply because our programs are not so effective as they ought to be. This is a great day for teachers, and it will be a day of great challenge and opportunity for the Church as a teaching institution.

THE MINISTER'S RESPONSIBILITY

An Oxford professor makes the judgment that in the Victorian Age, the Congregationalists made the greatest contribution to the serious education of the congregation.* He says that when R. W. Dale attacked the theology of original depravity in the chapel of Carr's Lane, Birmingham, in 1855, he made no attempt to simplify his language in discussing this rather difficult doctrine. Chadwick is of the opinion that had this same sermon been preached in an Anglican, a Roman Catholic, or a Methodist place of worship, most of the congregation would have gone to sleep. Yet at Carr's Lane, the result was excitement and almost an alarm that turned into panic. He says, "The congregation was like one great Bible class; there was a Bible open in almost every hand."

The modern minister is not likely to meet this kind of response in very many places. Yet, we must take more seriously our tasks as theological teachers, and we must be responsible for defining the great words of the Christian vocabulary. It is all very well to talk about the modern lack of

* Owen Chadwick, *The Victorian Church*, Oxford, 1966.

interest in such words as grace, sin, salvation, or redemption. Let us face the fact that there are no other words to say what these words say and that the only solution to the problem is to help our people learn the meaning of these great words. Any man who stays in one pulpit for a number of years ought to be ashamed if at the end of that time, his congregation is no more theologically aware than it was at the beginning.

This does not mean that we are to give our people certain definite, neat, theological answers to their important problems. The truth is that there are no pat answers to the real issues men raise, and they must always come to their solution indirectly. This has been said very clearly by the professor of preaching at Garrett Biblical Institute.* Professor Abbey writes this significant paragraph: " 'Its aim', as Ebeling writes, 'is, that there should be further proclamation . . . proclamation that has taken place is to become proclamation that takes place.' And, he adds, 'this does not normally happen through recitation.' It happens rather through direct address to the present hearer, showing him his own life in the light of the text. 'The sermon begins by announcing that John in prison was bewildered, and so are we; it continues by pointing that he took his trouble to Jesus, and so must we; and comes to its climax by reminding us that he got only an indirect answer, and so do we.' " (Paul Scherer). Yet, the minister as teacher is commissioned to point his hearers to the Great Teacher who meets us not in terms of pat answers but in the shedding of enough light on the path to enable us to take the next necessary steps.

Controversial issues will best be handled if there is a background of teaching involved. The church which gives the opportunity to explore background situations and discover

* Merrill R. Abbey, *The Word Interprets Us*, Abingdon, 1967, p. 27.

the real conditions will gradually create a strong body of the laity who can approach the hot issues with cool spirit. In the days of social tension and conflict, the church that has never faced its people with social and economic controversy always finds itself in trouble. This is the church where the split in the congregation occurs and sometimes a separation. The congregation, however, that has been in the habit of facing difficult questions both through the preached word from the pulpit and the careful study of the situation in small discussion groups will not be duly undisturbed. It has been my observation in these latter days that where the Birch Society, for example, managed to splinter the Christian fellowship, it was able to infiltrate only a people that had never been prepared to think through a Christian approach to Birchism or any other extremism. One of the most encouraging things to observe is a Christian Church that thrives and grows strongly on controversy rather than seeking security by clamping the lid down tight on it.

Thus when a group of youthful pickets appeared in the morning service to protest the minister's point of view on Vietnam, they were invited to remain after the service and the congregation was asked to remain and hear what they had to say. This was the minister as teacher at his best, and this spirit ought to characterize all congregations.

Nor should the minister assume that teaching is a one-way proposition. He needs to learn from his people as much as they need to learn from him. He needs to know more about the layman's problems and try to get the view of society from the man sitting in his congregation. This was the prophet's task according to Ezekiel, but to sit where they sit is the first duty of the minister as teacher.

THE TEACHING ART

Walter Prescott Webb, one-time president of the American Historical Association, said that there is something historically naughty about good writing and that "a great gulf exists between truth and beauty and the scholar who attempts to bridge it deserves to fall in and drown." He went on to say that "the real scholar must choose truth and somehow it is better if it is made so ugly that nobody could doubt its virginity." There are those who think that this is an apt description of scholarly teaching and the scholarly approach to any subject. If it should become interesting to anybody, then the man deserves the term "popularizer" and that is the next thing to saying that he is a charlatan. My own belief is that only dull people will accept this nonsense and that a survey of those who have made the great discoveries of mankind will reveal that when a new idea bursts upon the mind, it is about the most exciting thing that ever happens. To describe it in a boring, tiresome manner is impossible.

It is the mistaken idea that the scholarly approach must be dull that so often gives a man the wrong attitude toward preaching. One of the great mistakes we make is to assume that the professional teacher can transfer his skills over into the realm of preaching and that it will be well accepted. This is not true. These are two disciplines, and while good preaching will aways teach and good teaching once in a while forgets itself and preaches, we should never expect to be able to apply the techniques of one to the other with any satisfactory result.

Preaching has always the element of proclamation, and the sermon is an announcement of something that has happened and is happening. There is always in it a "thus saith the

Lord" element. When it lacks that we know that something has gone out of the pulpit. The attitude of the teacher is more of letting the exploration of an idea lead us where it will. While a sermon must have this spirit within it also, it never ends there. Teaching is the spirit of inquiry, and preaching is more the spirit of witness.

Indeed, one of the things that is wrong with our preaching today is that we listen too seriously to articles written by teachers. They are quite willing to pronounce judgment on public discourse of any kind as if their techniques are to be applied universally. Let the young preacher understand their limitations. But the preacher must always respect the teacher even if the teacher does not always respect or understand the preacher's art.

The great physicist, Niels Bohr, one time said that his problem was never to speak more clearly than he could think. This is our problem, and there is more than a half truth in the old admonition that if you want to really learn something then teach it. Gradually as we must arrange our thoughts in order to share them with other men, we face the necessity of clarifying some points which are vaguely understood but never sharply defined. This is another reason why it is a good idea to speak a sermon aloud as we prepare it, rather than simply think it through in our minds without verbalization.

The good teacher must never give the impression that he is putting boundaries around certain subjects and labeling some areas of thought as no-man's-land. Good teaching is always a willingness to examine any proposition and follow any clue even when it seems to lead into very unsavory places. For the Christian finally is free and his faith is fervent when he dares to examine any proposition as honestly as he is able. The parents who want their children guarded from the seamy side of life and who prefer to send them to schools where they shall be taught only "Christian teaching" are on a false path and do their children much harm. The humorous but usually pathetic sight of young people losing their religion in college is due usually to overzealous parents who thought they were making Christians of their offspring by protecting them. The minister as a teacher must be unshockable, and no man should doubt that his heresy shall receive an honest consideration when it is raised within the Church.

In the third century one of the great Christian scholars and teachers was Origen. A student said about his teaching, "No subject was forbidden us, nothing hidden or inaccessible. We were allowed to become acquainted with every doctrine, barbarian or Greek, with things spritual and secular, divine and human, traversing with all confidence and investigating the whole circuit of knowledge and satisfying ourselves with full enjoyment of the pleasures of the soul." You can hardly find a better description of what Christian teaching ought to be. I can well recall that one of the most disarming experiences in college was listening to a teacher who was an acknowledged churchman, and finding him not only willing but anxious to examine anything we had to offer. The minister ought to be that kind of man.

We have probably underestimated the human desire to know and learn. Education is discovering that children are so anxious to learn that we have held them back with our systems. Francis Keppel, the United States Commissioner of Education, wrote some time ago about experimental and creative schools where two- and three-year-old youngsters learned to read and write, where first graders learned the fundamentals of algebra, where second and third graders became familiar with relativity and physics, and where fourth and fifth graders learned to employ "set theory" in mathematics. This seems to indicate that our children in our church schools are quite capable of something more than just being entertained for an hour on Sunday morning.

One of the most exciting things we can see in our time is the hunger on the part of adults to learn. In many a community the evening adult program is one of the most exciting things happening. We ought to be more familiar with it as churchmen. We ought, also, to apply some of the lessons to our own work, and the churches should be night schools where subjects are offered not available anywhere else. When Frank Laubach began his great career of teaching people to read and setting free the illiterates of the world, he assumed that reading in itself was a good thing. But since they had to learn to read something, it might as well be something biblical and Christian. This the Church must do in its educational programs. There may be some objection that we are not equipped to do this job without the expenditure of huge sums of money. I do not think this is true.

Buckminster Fuller reported a study made in the early 1950's to determine what schools were producing great scientists.* Interestingly enough, it was not the California Institute of Technology nor the Massachusetts Institute of Technology and they were not even included in the first twenty schools. Reed College was the top United States source of first-rank scientists. Fuller said that more graduates from small liberal arts colleges became great scientists than were produced by the powerful scientific establishments. When the National Science Foundation asked the "breakthrough" scientists what was outstanding in their educational experience, they almost always answered, "Intimate association with a

* *Saturday Review,* Nov. 12, 1966.

great, inspiring teacher." I knew it was true in my own life
that great teachers were everything. I assumed that this
would be true for liberal arts students, but that it should also
be true for science majors is startling and significant. This
means that the essential equipment can be produced without
great cost, but that the most significant thing is the teacher.
He cannot be produced with money in any case, and he is
always a gift from God. In other words, the Church as a
teaching institution is able to do the important work it
would like to do if it can find leaders who know something
about the art of teaching.

In the midst of all our talk about relaxation and peace of
mind, it is still true that men need to feel they are stretching
themselves toward goals that are significant. Like St. Paul we
need to be reaching forth to those things which are before us.
This is not a matter of a particular age, but it is simply a
matter of being alive. The minister as teacher wants his congregation to feel dissatisfied with childish ideas of God and to
be ashamed of immature concepts of religion. For the saints
always seemed to assume there was so much more ahead than
they had ever experienced, and like the scientist who believes
he has touched only the shore of the sea of knowledge, so the
saint felt that he has barely touched the hem of His garment.

President Sachar of Brandeis University said he would not
stay too much longer as he thought the institution needed a
younger president. But he added that he would always be
around in some capacity because he had put too much into
Brandeis to desert it. He spoke of some of the joys of teaching, such as watching James "Scotty" Reston, the *New York
Times* columnist, develop into a first-rate political commentator and remember that he had taught this man a history course at Illinois years ago. He spoke of other men who

had been his students, and he remarked that when he asked one student what she had gotten out of Brandeis, she had replied, "You made me stretch." That, he thought, was the main objective of a university. And it might be added that this is one of the main objectives of a church, and the teaching function must be undergirded and inspired by the minister.

We have been altogether too willing to settle for too little. Sarah Shepherd, the associate superintendent of schools in St. Louis, commented some time ago on the weakness of teaching by I.Q. When she was asked what she meant, she replied with a little story. A teacher was working with a girl who had an I.Q. of 119, so when the teacher called on Mary, if a quick response was not forthcoming she would usually say, "Come on, Mary, you can do this. You have to think. You know how we worked at this last week." Here she was pushing and stimulating a student she knew had capacity. But when she called on Charles who had an I.Q. of 71 and he only grunted and gave no answer, she would say, "That's fine, son. We are glad you are here. Be sure to be here tomorrow. We are going to move the piano; you can water the flowers and clean the erasers." This is teaching by I.Q. which Dr. Shepherd says is not to be encouraged.

The Church has been too willing to assume that anything disturbing must be hidden from the people. We have had a tendency to believe that above all else we must not cause doubt in the minds of our congregation. I have known a few men who took intense delight in putting everything negatively and upsetting established faith, and I never thought they served the church very well. But the other side of the picture is no better. Indeed, in some ways it is more dangerous. For actually, faith that is worth anything must spring from doubt. The art of teaching is the art of struggling through all kinds of complex and seemingly contradictory propositions in order to come at long last to a solid foundation of conviction upon which a man can stand.

If we assume that all of us are to some extent prisoners, then our message must be one of deliverance. But liberation is never a camouflage of the prison. It is being captured by the spirit of One who "sets the prisoner free." The man who has never had to wrestle with the demons of doubt for his faith, is never adequately prepared for the conflicts of life all must face. The art of great teaching is to lead people through the valley of the shadow of doubt without fearing evil.

More than thirty years ago, Burris Jenkins preached a sermon entitled "Undaunted by Decembers" which was based on the quatrain:

> Undaunted by Decembers
> The sap is faithful yet.
> The giving earth remembers,
> And only men forget.

This is faith at its best, and this is the quality of the mind of the Christian who has faced the worst with open eyes and come finally to the best.

Good teaching is not necessarily presenting an exhaustive study of the subject. It is not bringing before people every possible instance and fact. It is always selection, and as Macaulay one time put it, the best historians are those "which exhibit such parts of the truth as most nearly produce the effect of the whole." This is sometimes called the scandal of particularity, but it is the Christian word that in one man's life and death and resurrection there is the clue to the whole.

The historian, says Barbara Tuchman,* cannot do without imagination. It is the small detail that reveals the situation. One of the best examples is Parkman whose *History of the West* remains unsurpassed and forever a classic. Long after more scholarly and academic studies have been forgotten under layers of dust on some library shelf, he will be read with appreciation and joy because he knew how to make the readers feel a situation. So the Bible becomes our great textbook with its power to illuminate places and eras through personal accounts and dramatic moments. And if we believe that what God has done for us in Christ is to give us the clue to the meaning of our lives, then we are of all men most blessed so far as teaching about life is concerned. For the great Teacher is a gift to our imagination, and in surrendering to his inspiration and charm, we begin the great adventure of making our life a triumph.

PREACHING AS THINKING

There was a cartoon showing a barefoot monk tramping out the grapes and muttering to himself, "Five years of moral theology, three years of homiletics, two years of patrology, four of church history . . ." The minister who has to fill the role of administrator often feels the same way and wonders why he must do these more prosaic and practical things when he has spent so much time studying intellectual disciplines. It is my conviction that the necessity of inhabiting different worlds is all to the good in the long run, but we must be aware that we do have a responsibility to be men of thought. A great deal of ministerial fist-pounding could be eliminated with no loss if in its place we put some fact-find-

* *Saturday Review*, Feb. 25, 1967.

ing exploration. Whenever the preacher leaves the judge's bench and takes the witness chair, it is good, and there is certainly a necessity for us to stand alongside our people. The preacher can make the mistake of trying to flog the will rather than feed the mind. Are we able to think as well as talk? is the question.

Dr. Carl Michalson, professor of theology at Drew Theological Seminary, was killed in an airplane crash in 1965. Just before he left to take that fatal flight, he had written a note to himself and left it on his desk. It read, "Take no dates from now on. Stay at desk and think." It would be a good thing for every one of us to write such notes to ourselves often. An important part of our ministry must be not only organizing our material into proclamation form but thinking through hard questions to discuss with our people, not from the pulpit, but from the round table. We shall not strive after the title of intellectual, but we shall certainly be far from a satisfactory ministry until we sharpen our minds to the limit of our capacity.

This does not mean that we must exchange the simple way of putting things with some academic obscurity. As our preaching should be direct and plain, so should our teaching. The late C. S. Lewis wrote with great insight and plainness and one time suggested that "An essential part of the ordination exam ought to be a passage from some recognized theological work set for translation into vulgar English." And then he came out with this clincher, "Failure on this paper should mean failure on the whole examination." That seems an extreme way to put it, but I find myself in complete agreement. It is a pity that the self-consciously intellectual preacher is so often left without hearers, and not for the reason he assumes. It is because plain men can spot in a very short time the pretender to profound knowledge which is really only muddy and obscure thinking.

John Wesley is a good example of a man who wanted to express his teachings in the language of the people, and he stated this purpose in the introduction to his sermons: "I design plain truth for plain people: therefore, . . . I abstain from all nice and philosophical speculations; from all perplexed reasonings. . . . I labor to avoid all words which are not easy to be understood, all which are not used in common language; and, in particular, those kinds of technical terms that so frequently occurred in Bodies of Divinity; those modes of speaking which men of reading are intimately acquainted with, but which to common people are an unknown tongue."*

Owen Chadwick in *The Victorian Church*† speaks of the dissenting ministers some of whom preferred obscurity and disliked the growth of the meetinghouse into a chapel and then into the church. He says, "By instinct they were men of the upper room." Granted that in our time this is a hard role to fill, but the upper room, whether it is the study in our home or the study in the church, had better be one of the places where we dwell regularly and long. For to think through the tangled philosophical jargon of the day and come to some clear gospel word about the real issues is our responsibility. I know of no other way to accomplish it than by long hours and lonely vigil.

Richard Baxter, the great Puritan preacher of the seventeenth century, said, "One can say more from the feeling and experience of his soul, than another can in a long time gather from his Books. And that which he saith will come warm to

* Robert C. Monk, *John Wesley: His Puritan Heritage*, Abingdon, 1966, p. 34.
† Oxford, 1966.

hearers in a more lively experimental manner, than usual carnal preachers speak." It may seem a little strange to modern ears to say that the preacher must be taught by the Holy Spirit. But when a man has been at this task for any length of time and considers it with any perception, the only way he can explain some of the happenings in his life and some of his insights is to assume they come from above. I believe with all my heart that if a man waits patiently and at the same time actively, he will be taught of these things by the Spirit who will guide him into the best means of communication.

Gamaliel Bradford wrote in his *Journal:* "I do not dare to read the New Testament for fear of awakening a storm of anxiety and self-reproach and doubt and dread of having taken the wrong path, of having been traitor to the plain and simple God." What this literary man was confessing as personal experience, a good teacher brings to bear on the conscience of every person. We come finally, however, to the realization that where we go wrong is in denying the plain and simple truths of God who has revealed Himself in Christ. The New Testament is a book unexcelled in bringing things to a head and confronting men with the necessity of an immediate choice.

In *The Goncourt Journal* for April 20, 1867, the Goncourt brothers made this entry: "This evening there was an unforgettable scene at the Pellegrini Hostel: rows of wild-looking, lice-ridden peasants seated on benches beneath a gas lamp which threw their heads into shadow and lit up their white open necked shirts; and, peeling off their stocking washing their feet in buckets, friars of the Pilgrim Trinity, dressed in red with white bands and aprons, carrying napkins over their arms like waiters, friars who were cardinals, princes, and young nobles, with varnished boots peeking out from under their robes and their emblazoned carriages waiting for them in the square. When each pair of filthy feet had been washed and dried the friar would take them in their hands, bend down and kiss them in two places.

"In our hearts of hearts, we felt a certain emotion at the sight of this impressive egalitarian ceremony, Catholic religion is a beautiful thing and a great source of humanity, and it irritates us to see men of culture and intelligence go down on their knees before the iron and marble religion of antiquity. Everything that is gentle and sensitive and movingly beautiful in modernity comes from Christ."

This is the testimony of an unbeliever driven to the strange confession that beauty is from Christ and that this dramatic ceremony broke through his veneer of cynicism and doubt. The Church grown wise from many centuries of experience knew that teaching can open the heart through the simplicity of drama. Let us beware lest we should become interested only in causes and not in persons. The minister as teacher learns that some of the greatest events happened when Jesus was with a small group, and so he must save an important place in his ministry for this function. Chesterton one time remarked that he never understood why a woman should think it was a great career to teach other people's children and a small career to teach her own. So the young man who feels called upon to teach will discover that in the church there is a congregation and through that congregation a community and a whole society.

Blessed is the minister for whom the word of Chaucer in the Prologue to the *Canterbury Tales* applies: "And gladly wolde he lerne, and gladly teche."

The minister as he functions in these several worlds knows that he is part of the mighty fellowship called the Church.

Always he is the servant of Christ and one among many brethren. We are not called to be *prima donnas* nor are we to be exalted by lesser men. But we must not lose the sense of the splendor of our calling. George S. Halas, long-time coach of a professional football team, the Chicago Bears, once wrote something about his work that will be helpful to us. "Football is a team game," he said. "There never has been a one-man team. But sometimes the addition of one man can make all the difference in a team." Let the minister remember this wise word.

DEMCO